Best Easy Day

Best Easy Day Hikes
Chapel Hill

Second Edition

Johnny Molloy

FALCONGUIDES

GUILFORD, CONNECTICUT

FALCONGUIDES®

An imprint of The Rowman & Littlefield Publishing Group, Inc.
4501 Forbes Blvd., Ste. 200
Lanham, MD 20706
www.rowman.com
Falcon and FalconGuides are registered trademarks and Make Adventure Your Story is a trademark of The Rowman & Littlefield Publishing Group, Inc.

Distributed by NATIONAL BOOK NETWORK

Maps by Melissa Baker

British Library Cataloguing in Publication Information available

Library of Congress Cataloging-in-Publication Data available

ISBN 978-1-4930-4852-6 (paper : alk. paper)
ISBN 978-1-4930-4853-3 (electronic)

♾️™ The paper used in this publication meets the minimum requirements of American National Standard for Information Sciences—Permanence of Paper for Printed Library Materials, ANSI/NISO Z39.48-1992.

Contents

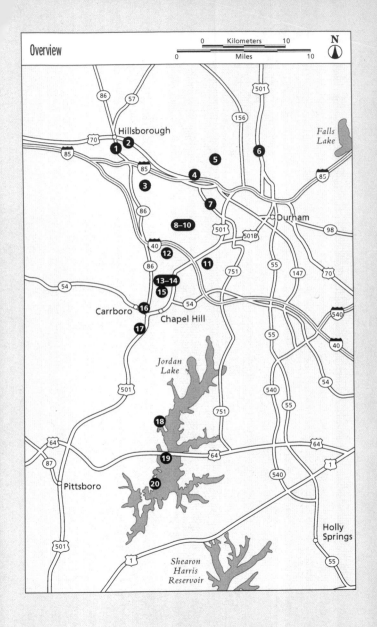

Kilometers
Miles
N

Acknowledgments

Thanks to all the people who helped me with this guide and the new edition as well. Thanks to my wife, Keri Anne, for her help and to Kelty for their tents, sleeping bags, and other equipment. Also, thanks to all the park personnel who answered my tireless questions while trying to manage the forests, parks, and preserves of greater Chapel Hill. The biggest thanks go to the local Chapel Hill hikers and trail builders, as well as those who visit this scenic slice of America, for without y'all there would not be trails in the first place.

Introduction

The surprising view extended far across Jordan Lake. I was hiking at appropriately named Vista Point Recreation Area. Below me stretched gorgeous lake waters bordered by verdant forest. Peninsulas jutted into the dammed impoundment of New Hope Creek. The underwhelmingly named Red Trail had led me to this panoramic view, one of the best easy day hikes in and around Chapel Hill. I mentally reflected on other best easy day hikes included in this guide. Nearby, Jordan Lake Educational State Forest presents information about forestry practices in a scenic setting that includes both creek and lake environments, a restored pine savanna, and an old homesite. The Pond Trail at Seaforth lives up to its name, visiting old farm ponds and traveling long boardwalks through wetlands along Jordan Lake. Back toward Chapel Hill, I recalled the fine greenway system enjoyed by its citizenry. The Morgan Creek Trail parallels a singing stream then circles atop a hill with good views. The natural surface Battle Branch Trail intertwines with a splashing creek through deep hills and surprising rock outcrops. The Bolin Creek Greenway makes the most of its valley setting as it winds through the city of the University of North Carolina Tar Heels. Speaking of UNC, Battle Park, scene of a fun and varied trek, is named for a former president and student at the esteemed university. Of course, Duke University cannot be overlooked in this guide, since three hikes travel through Duke Forest properties. These include the vertically varied Piney Mountain Hike, the flowery and geologically alluring Rhododendron Bluff Circuit, as well as the Big Bend Loop, which cuts through a "gorge"-ous segment of upper New Hope Creek. Up by Hillsborough, the Riverwalk links Gold

Park to downtown Hillsborough, along the gorgeous Eno River. The Eno River Valley is represented in other hikes, most of which are within the confines of Eno River State Park. The wildflower-rich Pump Station Loop meanders through a flowery flat then visits one of Durham's early water delivery systems. A hike in the Cabelands finds Eno Quarry, a 4-acre pond where you can also walk along the Eno River and gurgling Rhodes Creek.

In addition, what would Chapel Hill be without historical hiking? The Ayr Mount Poets Walk circles around a homestead from the early 1800s and visits bottomlands and waterways. The West Point hike at Eno Park not only ascends bluffs but also tours a collection of historic buildings, including one of the most famous mills in the Piedmont.

The laughing of children walking the trail brought me back to the here and now. These best easy day hikes of greater Chapel Hill are truly a treasure for locals and visitors coming to see this special slice of North Carolina. With this updated guide in hand and willing feet, you can explore greater Chapel Hill on the trails described within these pages. No matter where you go, the hikes will enhance your outdoor experience and leave you appreciating the natural splendors of the Piedmont. Enjoy.

The Nature of Chapel Hill and the Piedmont

Chapel Hill and the Piedmont's hiking grounds range from singletrack wooded trails along creeks and underneath resplendent forest to well-marked nature trails to strolls on asphalt interpretive paths. Hikes in this guide cover the gamut. While by definition a best easy day hike is not strenuous and generally poses little danger to the traveler, knowing

a few details about the nature of Chapel Hill and the Piedmont will enhance your explorations.

Weather

Chapel Hill certainly experiences all four seasons, though
it is a little long on summer. Summer can be very hot and
is the least popular hiking season. Thunderstorms can pop
up in the afternoons. I recommend hiking during the early
morning or late in the evening in summer. Hiking activity
increases when the first northerly fronts of fall sweep cool,
clear air across the Piedmont. Crisp mornings give way to
warm afternoons. Fall is drier than summer and is the driest
of all seasons. Winter can bring frigid subfreezing days and
chilling rains. On most winter days, however, a brisk hiking pace will keep you warm. Each cold month has several
days of mild weather. Spring is more variable. A warm day
can be followed by a cold one. Extensive spring rains bring
regrowth, but also keep hikers indoors. However, any avid
hiker will find more good hiking days than they will have
time to hike in spring and every other season.

Critters

Chapel Hill trail treaders will encounter mostly benign
creatures on these trails, such as deer, squirrels, wild turkeys,
a variety of songbirds, and rabbits—but especially deer.
More rarely seen (during the daylight hours especially) are
coyotes, raccoons, and opossums. Deer in some of the parks
are remarkably tame and may linger on or close to the trail
as you approach. When encountering any critter, keep your
distance and they will generally keep theirs.

Be Prepared

Hiking in the greater Chapel Hill area is generally safe. Still, hikers should be prepared, whether they are out for a short stroll at Ayr Mount or venturing into secluded sections of Jordan Lake State Recreation Area. Some specific advice:

- Know the basics of first aid, including how to treat bleeding, bites and stings, and fractures, strains, or sprains. Pack a first-aid kit on each excursion.

- Familiarize yourself with the symptoms of heat exhaustion and heat stroke. Heat exhaustion symptoms include heavy sweating, muscle cramps, headache, dizziness, and fainting. Should you or any of your hiking party exhibit any of these symptoms, cool the victim down immediately by rehydrating and getting him or her to an air-conditioned location. Cold showers also help reduce body temperature. Heat stroke is much more serious: The victim may lose consciousness and the skin is hot and dry to the touch. In this event, call 911 immediately.

- Regardless of the weather, your body needs a lot of water while hiking. A full 32-ounce bottle is the minimum for these short hikes, but more is always better. Bring a full water bottle, whether water is available along the trail or not.

- Don't drink from streams, rivers, creeks, or lakes without treating or filtering the water first. Waterways and water bodies may host a variety of contaminants, including giardia, which can cause serious intestinal unrest.

- Prepare for extremes of both heat and cold by dressing in layers.

- Carry a backpack in which you can store extra clothing, ample drinking water and food, and whatever goodies, like guidebooks, cameras, and binoculars, you might want. Consider bringing a GPS with tracking capabilities.

- Smart phone coverage is widespread, but you can never be absolutely sure until you are on location. Bring your device, but make sure you turn it off or to the vibrate setting while hiking. That way fellow hikers won't be disturbed by sudden rings of the phone. Also, your device can be used to locate your position should you become discombobulated.

- Keep children under careful watch. Trails travel along lakes and creeks, some of which are not recommended for swimming. Hazards along some of the trails include poison ivy, uneven footing, and potentially confusing user-created paths; make sure children don't stray from the designated route. Children should carry a plastic whistle; if they become lost, they should stay in one place and blow the whistle to summon help.

Zero Impact

Trails in the greater Chapel Hill area are well used year-round. We, as trail users, must be especially vigilant to make sure our passage leaves no lasting mark. Here are some basic guidelines for preserving trails in the region:

1. Pack out all your own trash, including biodegradable items like orange peels. You might also pack out garbage left by less considerate hikers.

2. Don't approach or feed any wild creatures—the ground squirrel eyeing your snack food is best able to survive if it remains self-reliant.

3. Don't pick wildflowers or gather rocks, shells, feathers, and other treasures along the trail, especially aboriginal and settler relics. Removing these items will only take away from the next hiker's experience and steal a piece of the historic puzzle that is Chapel Hill's past.

4. Avoid damaging trailside soils and plants by remaining on the established route. This is also a good rule of thumb for avoiding poison ivy and other common regional trailside irritants.

5. Be courteous by not making loud noises while hiking.

6. Many of these trails are multiuse, which means you'll share them with other hikers, trail runners, mountain bikers, and equestrians. Familiarize yourself with the proper trail etiquette, yielding the trail when appropriate.

7. Use outhouses at trailheads or along the trail.

Chapel Hill Area Boundaries and Corridors

For the purposes of this guide, best easy day hikes are confined to a one-hour drive from Chapel Hill, North Carolina.

Two major interstates and a major highway stretch out from Chapel Hill. Directions to trailheads are given from these interstates and arteries. They are I-40, I-85, and US 15/US 501.

Land Management

The following government organizations manage most of the public lands described in this guide, and can provide further information on these hikes and other trails in their service areas.

Jordan Lake State Recreation Area, 280 State Park Rd., Apex, NC 27523, (919) 362-0586, www.ncparks .gov

Eno River State Park, 6101 Cole Mill Rd., Durham, NC 27705, (919) 383-1686, www.ncparks.gov

Chapel Hill Parks and Recreation, 200 Plant Rd., Chapel Hill, NC 27514, (919) 968-2784, www.townof chapelhill.org

How to Use This Guide

This guide is designed to be simple and easy to use. Each hike is described with a map and summary information that delivers the trail's vital statistics including length, difficulty, fees and permits, park hours, canine compatibility, and trail contacts. Directions to the trailhead are also provided, along with a general description of what you will see along the way. A detailed route finder (Miles and Directions) sets forth mileages between significant landmarks along the trail.

Hike Selection

This guide describes trails that are accessible to every hiker, whether visiting from out of town or someone lucky enough to live in the Chapel Hill area. The hikes are no longer than 4.3 miles round-trip, and many are considerably shorter. They range in difficulty from flat excursions perfect for a family outing to more challenging treks. While these trails are among the best, keep in mind that nearby trails, often in the same park or preserve, may offer options better suited to your needs. I've sought to space hikes throughout the greater Chapel Hill area, so wherever your starting point, you'll find a great easy day hike nearby.

Difficulty Ratings

These are all easy hikes, but easy is a relative term. To aid in the selection of a hike that suits particular needs and abilities, each is rated easy, moderate, or more challenging. Bear in mind that even most challenging routes can be made easy by hiking within your limits and taking rests when you need them.

Easy hikes are generally short and flat, taking no longer than an hour to complete.

Moderate hikes involve increased distance and relatively mild changes in elevation, taking one to two hours to complete.

More challenging hikes feature greater distances and some steep stretches, generally taking longer than two hours to complete.

These are completely subjective ratings—what you think is easy is entirely dependent on your level of fitness and the adequacy of your gear (primarily shoes). If you are hiking with a group, you should select a hike with a rating that is appropriate for the least fit and prepared in your party.

Approximate hiking times are based on the assumption that on flat ground, most walkers average 2 miles per hour. Adjust that rate by the steepness of the terrain and your level of fitness (subtract time if you're an aerobic animal and add time if you're hiking with kids), and you have a ballpark hiking duration. Be sure to add more time if you plan to picnic or take part in other activities like bird watching or photography.

Trail Finder

Map Legend

85	Interstate Highway
70	US Highway
89	State Highway
1009	County/Forest Road
	Local Road
	Railroad
	Featured Trail
	Trail
	Boardwalk
	River/Creek
	Intermittent Stream
	Body of Water
	National Forest/Park
	State/County Park
	Sand
	Bench
	Boat Launch
	Bridge
	Building/Point of Interest
	Campground
	Dam
	Gate
P	Parking
	Peak/Summit
	Picnic Area
	Restroom
	Scenic View/Viewpoint
○	Town/City
10	Trailhead
	Waterfall

1 Riverwalk

This waterside trek starts at Hillsborough's Gold Park then leaves the city preserve to join the Riverwalk, crossing the Eno River twice. Continue winding through wooded lands along the waterway, stopping to soak in ample historical information about the area. The Riverwalk then penetrates the heart of Hillsborough and curves through River Park, nearing the farmers market and other downtown attractions. From there the trek continues down the Eno before turning around.

Distance: 3.0-mile balloon double loop
Hiking time: 1.5 hours
Difficulty: Easy
Trail surface: Asphalt, boardwalk, some pea gravel
Best season: Fall through spring and during events in Hillsborough
Other trail users: Joggers, bicyclers
Canine compatibility: Leashed dogs permitted

Fees and permits: None
Schedule: 8 a.m. to half hour after sunset
Maps: Riverwalk and Mountains-to-Sea Trail Network Map; USGS Hillsborough
Trail contacts: Eno River State Park, 6101 Cole Mill Rd., Durham, NC 27705, (919) 383-1686, www.ncparks.gov

Finding the trailhead: From exit 164 on I-85, north of Chapel Hill, head north on Churton Street to cross the Eno River at 1 mile and reach downtown Hillsborough. Continue straight for 0.1 mile then turn left on Margaret Lane and follow it 0.6 mile to turn left on Nash Street. Follow Nash Street downhill 0.2 mile to the Norfolk Southern Railroad tracks then veer left on Dimmocks Mill Road. Go under the railroad then make an immediate left into Gold Park, quickly reaching

The Hike

Hillsborough is yet another community that is returning to its river roots. As the United States became more auto based, many towns founded on waterways simply left the rivers to flow on unnoticed. However, Hillsborough has seen the value of the Eno River running directly through its downtown. Combined with the increased interest in greenways, what better place to put a paved trail than along the Eno River as it flows through downtown Hillsborough? Even better, why not create a riverside trail linking to city and state parks located astride the Eno? That is exactly what the town of Hillsborough did—and it has been a smashing success. Today the Riverwalk is used not only by hikers but also by parents with strollers, joggers, and tourists who find their way to this quaint Piedmont community, as well as folks taking a break from their businesses located downtown. Speaking of that, hikers can easily access businesses located directly off the Riverwalk. A pleasant afternoon will find patrons eating lunch in the parks and then walking it off.

The first part of the Riverwalk was opened in 2009 then expanded since then, continuing to stretch in both directions along the Eno River. Spur trails link to adjacent streets and neighborhoods. Interestingly, the Mountains-to-Sea Trail—North Carolina's master path running from the mountains to the ocean—uses the Riverwalk as it passes through here. Interpretive signage detailing the history of the area adds to the walk, as do a pair of bridges that cross the Eno River.

The hike starts at Gold Park, a fine little preserve with a mini network of trails as well as a dog park and play area for kids, then heads east along the Eno River, where it squeezes under a railroad trestle, crosses the river, and enters a 12-acre tract donated by Peggy Cates Bartow. An additional loop trail is located here in the streamside woods. Continuing on, walkers will view rock outcrops along the river and then cross the waterway yet again. Here they will reach downtown and accesses to businesses. The trail was designed to pass under a couple of roads then emerge at River Park, a pleasant place to relax and perhaps buy vegetables and other goodies at the farmers market in season.

Next, the Riverwalk leads over a rehabilitated stream, Stillhouse Branch, then by the former site of an Occoneechee Indian village that was reconstructed here but then moved to the local tribal center. Finally, the Riverwalk leaves downtown and heads along the Eno linking to the Historic Occoneechee Speedway trails. Expect the trail to continue in the future, and expect to have a fun walk along this path. I suggest incorporating activities located in downtown Hillsborough as part of your Riverwalk experience.

Miles and Directions

0.0 As you face the Gold Park picnic shelter, take the paved path to your right. Head toward the Eno River then quickly turn right, bridging a small unnamed creek. Ahead, pass a shortcut trail leaving left.

0.2 Turn left, heading downstream along the Eno River, as an extension of the Riverwalk heads right and links to Occoneechee Mountain State Park and its trails.

0.3 Pass the other end of the shortcut. Keep along the Eno, crossing the small unnamed stream again. A pair of paved spurs returns to the trailhead, which you can see across grassy Gold Park.

Riverwalk

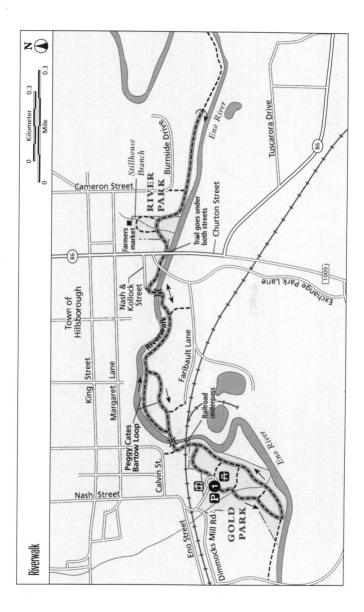

N

0   Kilometer   0.3
0   Mile   0.3

Town of Hillsborough

Nash Street

King Street

Margaret Lane

Calvin St.

Eno Street

Dimmocks Mill Rd.

P 1

GOLD PARK

Peggy Cates Bartow Loop

Railroad underpass

Faribault Lane

Riverwalk

Nash & Kollock Street

Eno River

Farmers market

Cameron Street

RIVER PARK

Stillhouse Branch

Burnside Drive

Eno River

Trail goes under both streets

Churton Street

Tuscarora Drive

86

86

1009

Exchange Park Lane

0.5 Walk beyond the last spur leading back to the Gold Park trailhead. Leave Gold Park and pass under a railroad bridge on a covered walkway, roofed to prevent debris from falling on walkers if a train is passing overhead. Just ahead, a spur trail leads left up to Calvin Street while the Riverwalk crosses the Eno River on a pedestrian bridge. Just ahead, stay left as you reach the Peggy Cates Bartow Loop. Continue downriver.

0.9 Pass the east end of the Peggy Cates Bartow Loop. Keep along the river toward downtown.

1.0 A spur goes right to Faribault Lane. Keep straight.

1.1 Cross back over the Eno on a bridge. A short spur leaves left to Nash and Kollock Street. Stay right here and descend to a boardwalk continuing along the Eno. Walk bottomland, passing under Exchange Park Lane and Churton Street. Enter River Park. Curve away from the water. A spur goes to the farmers market. Stay straight, then bridge Stillhouse Branch. Pass the former site of the reconstructed Occoneechee village.

1.4 Return to the Eno, leaving downtown behind.

1.5 Pass a spur going left to Cameron Street. Keep straight.

1.7 Turn around at a bridge. The trail will be expanded in the future but for now backtrack.

2.6 Pick up new trail, walking the other side of the Peggy Cates Bartow Loop.

3.0 Return to Gold Park, completing the hike.

2 Ayr Mount Poets Walk

Take a hike at a historic Hillsborough estate. Start your walk in sight of this brick plantation house from the early 1800s, then pass through the grounds to enter woods and find the Eno River. Soak in aquatic views as you travel wooded bottomland then rise back from the river. Come near a pond then circle around the front of this federal-style house, viewing it dead on. The last part goes along an ancient Indian trading path.

Distance: 1.0-mile loop
Hiking time: 1.0 hour
Difficulty: Easy
Trail surface: Natural
Best season: Year-round
Other trail users: History buffs
Canine compatibility: Leashed dogs permitted
Fees and permits: None to hike, fee to tour house
Schedule: Jan, Feb, Nov, Dec 9 a.m.–5 p.m.; Mar, Oct 9 a.m.– 6 p.m.; Apr, May, Aug, Sept 9 a.m.–7 p.m.; June, July 9 a.m.– 9 p.m.
Maps: Ayr Mount Poets Walk; USGS Hillsborough
Trail contacts: Classical American Homes Preservation Trust, 69 E. 93rd St., New York, NY 10128, (919) 732-6886, www.classical americanhomes.org

Finding the trailhead: From exit 164 on I-85, north of Chapel Hill, head north on Churton Street to cross the Eno River at 1 mile and reach downtown Hillsborough. Continue straight for 0.1 mile more then turn right on King Street. Follow it 0.2 mile then turn left on Saint Marys Road. Follow Saint Marys Road for 0.7 mile to reach the Ayr Mount entrance on your right. Official trailhead address is 376 Saint Marys Rd. Trailhead GPS: N36 4.7915', W79 5.1495'

The Hike

Triangle residents are lucky to have such a preserved house as Ayr Mount, the home of Scottish immigrant William Kirkland. The classical brick manse exudes regal simplicity. The interior's high ceilings and elaborate wood and plaster work of the house has made it one of the Piedmont's most important historic structures. Situated in the town of Hillsborough and listed on the National Register of Historic Places, Ayr Mount was home to William Kirkland and his descendants for nearly 200 years before being sold in 1985 and restored. Today Ayr Mount joins the ranks of fine houses maintained by the Classical American Homes Preservation Trust. You can tour the inside of the house to see the woodwork and antiques used by the Kirklands, as well as other significant furnishings.

Though the original plantation covered over 500 acres, 60 of those acres are still part of the greater plantation property and are the setting for this walk. In earlier times Mr. Kirkland's plantation produced wheat and cotton on the slopes above and bottoms along the Eno River. Several outbuildings once surrounded the brick home we see today, including a stone barn, slave quarters, poultry and milk barns, an icehouse, and a smokehouse.

William Kirkland emigrated from Ayr, Scotland, when he was twenty-one years old and became a trader, with a store in Hillsborough. His honest dealings and business savvy grew his bank account. He became part of the fabric of Hillsborough, living in the town for twenty-six years before he built this stately home, which he named for his homeland. Being from the mercantile class, it was only natural that his home was located along the Old Indian Trading Path, a route used by pre-Columbian natives linking villages in the Piedmont and beyond, as well as early Piedmont settlers. Mr. Kirkland enjoyed Ayr Mount for over two decades before passing away in 1836 at the age of sixty-eight.

The hiking trail is what makes this home so unusual. Most restored homes do not include trails with them, but Ayr Mount does. In their own words, the preservation trust does so for "open space preservation, watershed protection, and ecological recreation." Today you can park near the house then follow the marked trail past a picnic area. Walkers can admire the Ayr Mount grounds and landscaping before descending into natural woods and finding the free-flowing Eno River. Here you can walk along the waterway and look across at more preserved land containing trails—the Historic Occoneechee Speedway—site of one of the early NASCAR tracks and also owned by the preservation trust.

After your woodland experience the trail rises back into mown fields and forest and passes a pond. It then comes alongside the Old Indian Trading Path, where you can walk beside this gullied trail where thousands from previous centuries tromped. Here you can also gain a front-on view of Ayr Mount, soaking in the grounds and grandeur of this Piedmont treasure, before returning to the trailhead.

Miles and Directions

0.0 From the parking area, with Ayr Mount to your left, you will see a sign leading visitors left to the house tour and right to Poets Walk. Take the Poets Walk and shortly pass the home cemetery. Ayr Mount rises to your left. Just ahead, meander through the shaded picnic area in a mix of trees and fields.

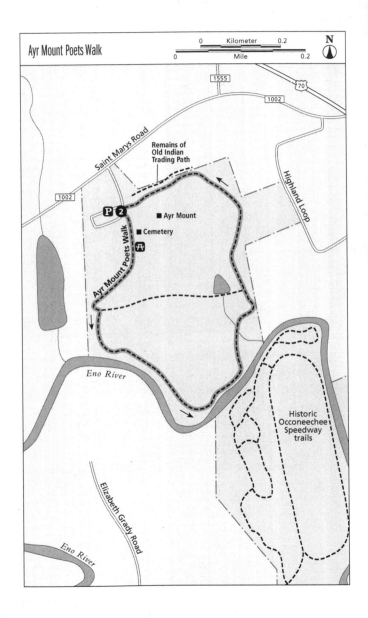

Ayr Mount Poets Walk

0   Kilometer   0.2

0   Mile   0.2

N

1555

70

1002

Saint Marys Road

Remains of
Old Indian
Trading Path

Highland Loop

1002

P 2

Ayr Mount

Cemetery

Ayr Mount Poets Walk

Eno River

Historic
Occoneechee
Speedway
trails

Elizabeth Grady Road

Eno River

0.2 A shortcut trail leads left toward the property pond. Keep straight, entering full-blown woods. Soon come alongside the Eno River. Pass spur trails leading to the river.

0.4 Open onto a field then come close along the river. Bluffs rise across the water. River shoals dance below. Turn away from the river in a mix of field and forest.

0.7 Reach the other end of the shortcut and come near the pond. Keep straight, rising toward Ayr Mount.

0.8 Top out then curve left, walking in front of Ayr Mount. Look for the gullied remains of the ancient trading path to your right.

1.0 Return to the trailhead, completing the hike.

3 Stony Creek Hike

This hike explores Stony Creek, the aquatic pulse of Duke Forest's Edeburn Division. Head up old Eno Road, crossing Stony Creek by bridge. Flat Rock Trail begins the loop where you cross Stony Creek at a large level outcrop. From there, wander up the watershed, crossing Stony Creek and its tributaries. Climb to make a loop atop Oak Hill, where you can see stone remains of an old homesite. Your return trip passes pine plantations and other evidences of a managed forest.

Distance: 4.1-mile balloon double loop
Hiking time: 2.0–2.5 hours
Difficulty: Moderate
Trail surface: Gravel and natural surface
Best season: Spring through fall
Other trail users: None
Canine compatibility: Leashed dogs permitted

Fees and permits: None
Schedule: Sunrise to sunset
Maps: Duke Forest Edeburn Division; USGS Hillsborough
Trail contacts: Office of the Duke Forest, Duke University, PO Box 90332, Durham, NC 27708, (919) 613-8013, www.duke forest.duke.edu

Finding the trailhead: From exit 263 on I-40, west of Durham, take New Hope Church Road north. Follow it for 2.1 miles to Gate 28 of the Edeburn Division of Duke Forest, on your left. There is limited roadside shoulder parking, but you can park in the grassy clearing under power lines just before the trailhead. Trailhead GPS: N36 1.860', W79 3.633'

The Hike

Duke Forest Teaching & Research Library, established in 1931, is divided into divisions, each division representing a tract of forest scattered around the capital region. Most of the divisions are located between Durham, Chapel Hill, and Hillsborough. The private forests, most parcels of which are open to the public, are used as living laboratories to further forestry practices in the Piedmont. This particular tract, formerly known as the Eno Tract, was renamed for Judson Edeburn, who managed the Duke Forest system from 1978 until 2014. This lesser-visited tract covers 490 acres and serves to mitigate fast runoff of the Stony Creek watershed from surrounding suburbs.

Stony Creek, a tributary of the Eno River, flows easterly through the Edeburn Division, picking up tributaries of its own along the way. The aptly named stream sports a rocky bed as it winds between pine- and oak-clad hills. Your first view of the creek comes as you walk Eno Road. Duke Forests offer a combination of gravel forest roads and singletrack foot trails for hikers. All forest roads are gated; vehicle use is only by forest management personnel. Eno Road crosses Stony Creek then rises to a wooded hill and trail intersection. The loop portion of this hike leaves right on the Flat Rock Trail. Back down you go, meeting Stony Creek again. Here you find the reason for this trail's name, as a wide rock slab stretches along Stony Creek. This makes for a fine relaxing locale, where the stream sings for streamside visitors. Rock-hop the creek, an easy proposition save for after storms and wet winter periods. Cruise up a streamside flat. Stay away from the spur path leading up to Hoot Owl Drive.

Beyond the intersection, the hike wanders hilly woods, going where you think it won't or shouldn't go. Truth is, the path is meandering woods inside the Edeburn Division boundaries, maximizing the hiking acreage. Suddenly, you meet the Norfolk Southern Railroad then turn away, passing through some tree-covered dug lands, whose purpose is lost to time. The altered terrain may have been part of a farm operation, or dug to provide fill for the adjacent railroad. After leaving this spot, cross Stony Creek yet again without benefit of footbridge, then work your way up an unnamed tributary, marking the division between timbered and untimbered lands. The hike crosses this tributary (again, no bridge) then rises on Slick Ford Trail.

Here begins a second, smaller loop, climbing Oak Hill, the high point of the hike. Trail trekkers will find rock and stone remains of a homesite, ensconced in tall evergreens. This was likely the primary quarters back when the Stony Creek valley was farmed and grazed, in the pre–Duke Forest days. After this historic interlude you take doubletrack trail through differing stands of managed forest, from green, tightly grown pine plantations to ranks of regal oaks, back to the trailhead.

Miles and Directions

0.0 Head west from Gate 28 on gravel Eno Road, open only to forest personnel vehicles. Pass a memorial commemorating the renaming of the Edeburn Division. Continue in rich woods.

0.3 Bridge Stony Creek then rise westerly under sweetgum, oaks, and pine. Note the rock piles from cultivated land.

0.4 Reach a four-way intersection and hilltop. Turn right onto the Flat Rock Trail and descend.

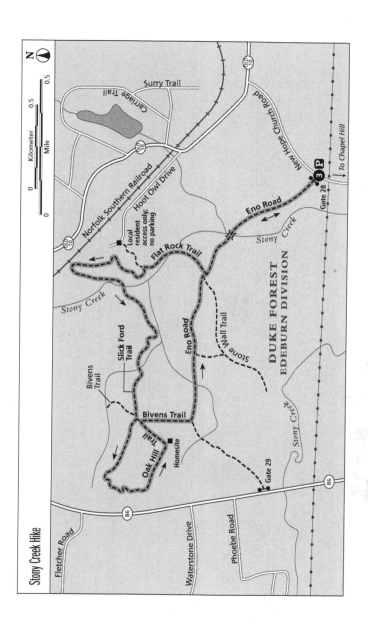

Stony Creek Hike

0.8 Reach gurgling Stony Creek at a wide rock slab. Rock-hop the stream.

0.9 Come to a trail intersection. Stay left as a trail leads right to Hoot Owl Drive, off which a bootleg user-created path (not shown on map) cuts back to the trailhead. Cruise wooded flats along Stony Creek then turn away from the stream.

1.3 Curve left upon nearing the Norfolk Southern Railroad tracks. Wind through dug lands pocked with trees and small, ephemeral wetlands.

1.5 Cross a now-smaller Stony Creek at a rocky rapid, an old ford site, without benefit of footbridge. The trail now runs along a tributary of Stony Creek, with timbered lands to your right and the tributary to the left.

1.9 Cross the unnamed tributary and climb, joining Slick Ford Trail.

2.1 Keep straight as doubletrack Bivens Trail leaves right. Just ahead, join the singletrack Oak Hill Trail leaving right as the doubletrack Bivens Trail leaves left. Wind through woods, gradually working uphill.

2.5 Top out on Oak Hill. Turn south. The trail widens.

2.8 Pass the stone foundation of a house in pines. Descend.

2.9 Turn right onto Bivens Trail, southbound.

3.1 Stay left, joining Eno Road, as a spur goes right to Gate 29. Head east.

3.4 Pass a spur leading right to Stone Wall Trail. Keep straight.

3.7 Reach the four-way intersection and hilltop. Keep straight on Eno Road, now backtracking.

4.1 Return to the trailhead, completing the hike.

4 Cabelands Hike

This is a fun and popular hike, sometimes almost too busy. Avoid this trek on Saturdays if possible. Start at Eno River State Park's Cabelands area and take the Cabelands Trail down toward the Eno to pick up the Eno Quarry Trail. Here you will cross historic Indian Fish Dam Road en route to Eno Quarry, a 4-acre tarn, popular with anglers and swimmers in season. Cross Rhodes Creek then circle around Eno Quarry. Next, head back to the Cabelands Trail where you travel along the Eno River, visiting historic Cabe Mill. The final part of the route leads back to the trailhead.

Distance: 2.3-mile double loop
Hiking time: 1.5 hours
Difficulty: Easy
Trail surface: Natural
Best season: Year-round, summer for swimming
Other trail users: Anglers, swimmers
Canine compatibility: Leashed dogs permitted
Fees and permits: None

Schedule: May–Sept 8:30 a.m.–8:30 p.m.; Mar, Apr, Oct 8:30 a.m.–7:30 p.m.; Nov 8:30 a.m.–6:30 p.m.; Dec, Jan, Feb 8:30 a.m.–6:30 p.m.
Maps: The Trails of Eno River State Park; USGS Northwest Durham, Hillsborough
Trail contacts: Eno River State Park, 6101 Cole Mill Rd., Durham, NC 27705, (919) 383-1686, www.ncparks.gov

Finding the trailhead: From exit 173 on I-85, northeast of Chapel Hill and west of downtown Durham, join Cole Mill Road northbound. Follow it 2.5 miles to turn left on Sparger Road. Follow Sparger Road for 1.2 miles to turn right on Howe Street. Follow Howe Street for 0.5 mile to turn right into the trailhead. If the busy parking lot is full, try another hike. Trailhead GPS: N36 2.395, W78 59 25.90

The Hike

Barnaby Cabe lent his name to this parcel on the south side of the Eno River. He settled here and became an active citizen, serving in the local militia and as a congressional representative. Ol' Barnaby Cabe built quite an operation, with his croplands and his gristmill, the remains of which you will walk by. He also left a family legacy through his three wives and nine daughters. Perhaps this is why the area is called the Cabelands. Long before Barnaby Cabe arrived here in the 1700s, local Indians were traversing the area via the Fish Dam Road, an aboriginal trace linking villages of the Occoneechee on the Eno River with natives on the Neuse River. Old Fish Dam Road was incorporated into colonial settler roads, and even streets of what became American towns in the area, though many of the avenues took newer, different names.

The start of this hike can be confusing as two trails side by side leave the parking area. One of them is the correct Cabelands Trail and the other heads to the Cabe-McCown Cemetery. Ahead, you cross a gullied, forgotten segment of Fish Dam Road that has reverted back to nature.

Then you come to Eno Quarry. It came to be when rock fill was needed for I-85 as it was being built through the Triangle. Superior Stone Company worked the quarry from 1961 to 1964. After the quarry was abandoned and the land returned to the owners, water slowly filled the void, mostly from underground, creating a 60-foot-deep, 4-acre pond, separated from adjacent Rhodes Creek by a man-made berm and from the Eno River by a narrow neck of land.

After returning to the Cabelands Trail, you hike alongside the Eno River and, before leaving the waterway, come to the site of the old Cabe Mill. The tailrace is the most visible feature of this mill, which was in operation during the late 1700s through early 1800s. After that, head back in the hills toward the parking area. It is fascinating to reflect how on this hike you get to see three bodies of water—Rhodes Creek, the pond of Eno Quarry, and the Eno River—as well as multiple historic sites, all in a short span.

Miles and Directions

0.0 From the Howe Street parking area, take the Cabelands Trail north just a short distance then come to a trail intersection. Head left, still on the Cabelands Trail. The trail narrows. Quickly dip and cross a small tributary of the Eno on a boardwalk. The trail is rocky and rooty.

0.4 Cross the old Cabe Mill access road just before coming to a trail intersection. Head left on the Eno Quarry Trail. Step over the historic Fish Dam Road twice in succession. It is an eroded roadbed now growing over with trees, making it hard to believe that 100 years ago this was a significant area thoroughfare.

0.8 Rock-hop Rhodes Creek then come to the trail circling around Eno Quarry. Head left and begin traversing a berm separating Eno Quarry from Rhodes Creek. Cross over a wetland after curving around the quarry pond via boardwalks.

0.9 Come to the ranger quarry access road. Rangers patrol the quarry looking for drunken swimmers during the warm season. Continue curving around the quarry, passing over irregular, non-natural piles of debris atop which trees are now growing.

1.0 Meet the Laurel Bluffs Trail. It leaves left 1.5 miles to reach the Pleasant Green trailhead on Pleasant Green Road. Our hike heads right, traversing a strip of land between the quarry and the Eno River. Curve up Rhodes Creek, completing the quarry circuit. Backtrack toward the Cabelands Trail.

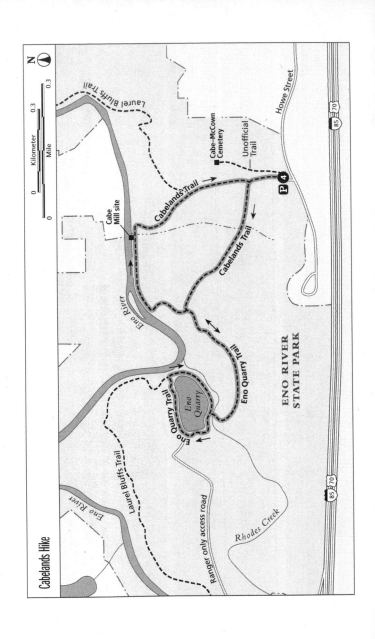

Cabelands Hike

N

ENO RIVER STATE PARK

Eno River

Laurel Bluffs Trail

Cabelands Trail

Cabe Mill site

Cabe-McCown Cemetery

Unofficial Trail

P 4

Howe Street

85 US 70

Cabelands Trail

Eno Quarry Trail

Eno Quarry

Eno Quarry Trail

Laurel Bluffs Trail

Eno River

Ranger only access road

Rhodes Creek

85 US 70

0   0.3   Kilometer
0   0.3   Mile

1.5 Head left on the Cabelands Trail, dropping toward the Eno River. Hike along a wide segment of the Eno.

1.8 Hike along a tailrace and the Cabe Mill site before turning away from the Eno River. Travel up a streambed after crossing a pair of wooden hiker bridges.

2.0 Stay straight as the Laurel Bluffs Trail leaves left for Cole Mill Road.

2.3 Return to the trailhead after completing the Cabelands loop portion of the hike and backtracking a short distance.

5 Pump Station Loop

This circuit hike travels hills down to flats along the Eno River, where it then explores what is considered the best wildflower area at Eno River State Park. From there, come alongside the river to find remains of an old pump station that served the city of Durham, providing water a century back. Explore these ruins then rise back to uplands along Nancy Rhodes Creek, with more wildflowers in season. The final part of the hike returns through hilly pine woods.

Distance: 1.5-mile loop
Hiking time: 1.0 hour
Difficulty: Easy
Trail surface: Natural
Best season: Year-round
Other trail users: History buffs, wildflower lovers
Canine compatibility: Leashed dogs permitted
Fees and permits: None
Schedule: May–Sept: 7:30 a.m.–9:30 p.m.; Mar, Apr, and Oct: 7:30 a.m.–8:30 p.m.; Nov: 7:30 a.m.–7:30 p.m.; Dec, January, and February: 7:30 a.m.–6:30 p.m.
Maps: The Trails of Eno River State Park; USGS Northwest Durham
Trail contacts: Eno River State Park, 6101 Cole Mill Rd., Durham, NC 27705, (919) 383-1686, www.ncparks.gov

Finding the trailhead: From exit 173 on I-85, west of downtown Durham, join Cole Mill Road northbound. Follow it 2.5 miles to turn right on Rivermont Road. Follow Rivermont Road for 0.3 mile to the trailhead on your left, just after Rivermont Road turns to gravel. Parking is on the shoulder. Trailhead GPS: N36 3.529', W78 58.153'

The Hike

The city of Durham was founded in 1869. The growing town had a rising demand for a reliable water system. In 1886 a man named A. H. Howland was contracted to build a pump station and dam to provide the desired aqua to Durham. Down on the Eno River, a dam was built not to provide a water supply but to provide waterpower to pump water from yet another dam on adjacent Nancy Rhodes Creek, a tributary of the Eno. It was the water from Nancy Rhodes Creek that Durham would consume. The power derived from the Eno River Dam would move the water from the Eno up to a place called Huckleberry Hill, where there was a reservoir. From this elevated reservoir, water would be gravity fed to the city of Durham.

By April 1888 the water system was operating. However, problems were immediate. A lack of water pressure and inconsistent flow were the primary complaints. Then a series of fires in 1894 and 1895 underscored the fact that the water system had insufficient pressure for firefighters to combat city blazes. And then there was a little problem about the water being muddy and sometimes containing fish. A remedy was sought, and a filtration system was installed, yet inconsistent service continued.

The city of Durham knew when to cut their losses and moved on to develop other water sources, though the Eno River/Nancy Rhodes Creek plant continued as a backup before being abandoned. Today you can see the ruins of the dam on Nancy Rhodes Creek, as well as a circular pond gouged out from the dam's overflow chute. Nearby is the foundation of the pump house on the Eno River. The largest ruins are from the large filtration plant near the dam.

Amateur archaeologists can spend quite a while examining the stone, brick, and metal remains of this early water system. Remember to leave your discoveries at the site, allowing others to enjoy a similar experience.

There is more to this hike in addition to the ruins of the pump house. The trails are well marked and maintained and are pleasant to hike. The grades are moderate as you descend to the river, and once beside the Eno, the waterside flats are gorgeous, backed with rising hills. Access to the river is easy. Just remember to build in some time to explore the pump station ruins. Your climb out along Nancy Rhodes Creek is not bad either. Upon reaching Rivermont Road, cross Nancy Rhodes Creek using the road bridge. From there the loop reenters woods and gets back on a hiker path leading back to the trailhead.

Miles and Directions

0.0 Leave the shoulder parking on Rivermont Road. Pass around a pole gate, joining the Pump Station Trail. Go just a short distance and meet the other end of the loop. Keep straight, passing under pines on a wide, easy trail.

0.2 Walk under a power line clearing.

0.4 Reach a trail intersection. Here the Laurel Bluffs Trail leaves left toward the Cabelands. Our hike turns right, following the Laurel Bluffs Trail along the Eno River in wooded riverside flats rich with beech. Now the Eno River splits around an island. Look for wildflowers aplenty in April. Mountain laurel blooms later in the season.

0.6 The flat is squeezed in by a bluff. The trail goes alongside the river, shaded by sycamore, river birch, and ironwood.

0.8 Curve away from the river to bridge Nancy Rhodes Creek. Note the small circular pond just before the bridge, created from the splashing waters of the dam overflow chute. The

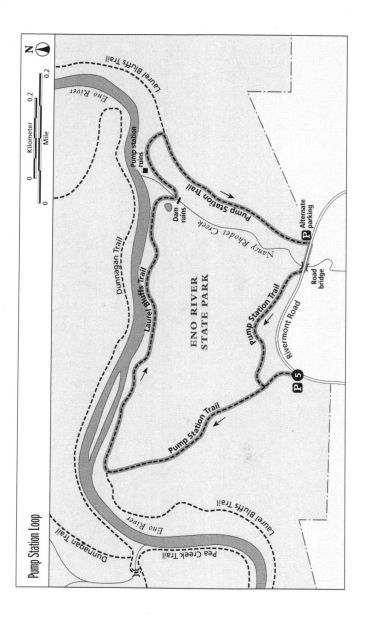

Pump Station Loop

N

ENO RIVER
STATE PARK

Eno River

Laurel Bluffs Trail

Dunnagan Trail

Pump station
ruins

Dam ruins

Nancy Rhodes Creek

Pump Station Trail

Laurel Bluffs Trail

Pump Station Trail

P Alternate parking

Road bridge

Rivermont Road

P 5

Pump Station Trail

Eno River

Pea Creek Trail

Laurel Bluffs Trail

Dunnagan Trail

Kilometer
0   0.2

Mile
0   0.2

partially standing high dam walls along Nancy Rhodes Creek rise just upstream of the bridge. User-created trails split off, exploring the dam area.

0.9 Reach the pump station area after heading downstream along Nancy Rhodes Creek. To your left stands the foundation of the pump station, and the filtration building is nearby. The Laurel Bluffs Trail leaves left toward Guess Road. Take time to explore this area, then resume the loop, ignoring the ranger access road.

1.0 Pass through a power line clearing, rising away from the Eno River and the pump station ruins. Come near the dam on Nancy Rhodes Creek. User-created trails lead right to the dam, while the official trail reenters woods, climbing along Nancy Rhodes Creek.

1.3 Come to Rivermont Road and alternate parking. Turn right on the road, cross Nancy Rhodes Creek, then reenter woods, back on footpath. Climb, continuing on Pump Station Trail to finish the loop portion.

1.5 Return to the trailhead, completing the hike, after backtracking just a short distance.

6 West Point on the Eno

This adventure explores human and natural history along the Eno River. The Laurel Cliff Trail leaves a collection of impressive historic wooden structures to climb a bluff above the Eno River and meet the Buffalo Trail. From there you drop to the deep Sennett Hole then traverse rock- and evergreen-laced bluffs overlooking the waterway. From there you pass an old milldam then come to iconic West Point on the Eno Mill.

Distance: 1.5-mile loop
Hiking time: 1.0–1.5 hours
Difficulty: Easy
Trail surface: Natural
Best season: Year-round
Other trail users: Anglers, history buffs
Canine compatibility: Leashed dogs permitted

Fees and permits: None
Schedule: 8 a.m. to dark
Maps: West Point on the Eno; USGS Northwest Durham
Trail contacts: West Point on the Eno Park, 5101 N. Roxboro Rd., Durham, NC 27704, (919) 471-1623, http://durhamnc.gov/

Finding the trailhead: From exit 176 on I-85, take US 501 north for 3.3 miles to West Point on the Eno Park. The left turn into the park is at a traffic light. Drive the one-way park road to circle past the mill and reach the barn-like picnic shelter after 0.3 mile. Official address is 5101 N. Roxboro Rd. Trailhead GPS: N36 4.178', W78 54.598'

The Hike

This 388-acre city of Durham park is situated where old Roxboro Road once crossed the Eno River at Shoemakers Ford. This ford was a strategic location to build a mill. Nearby residents flocked here to have their corn and wheat ground. The first area mill was built in 1752 by Michael Synott. Mr. Synott sold out to the Abercrombie brothers in 1780, but left a corrupted version of his name at the Sennett Hole, where he purportedly drowned trying to retrieve his hidden gold during a flood. The Abercrombies moved the operation to a better site just downstream and built what became known as West Point on the Eno Mill. For 160 years this mill operated, though it changed hands numerous times. One notable owner was a man named Herbert Sims, who was a lawman, county politician, and major landowner during the early to mid-1800s. It was during Mr. Sims's time, 1839 it was, that a post office was set up at the mill site, which had become a regular community with a general store, blacksmith shop, cotton gin, and even a whiskey still. This spot was the last and most westerly stop for the US mail between Roxboro and Durham; thus the community became known as West Point.

In 1888 the mill fell into the hands of Hugh Mangum, known as one of the earliest photographers of Durham. Today a museum of photography stands on the site's park grounds, featuring Mr. Mangum's work. There are also many pictures of the West Point Mill there. He bought the 1840s house that still stands on the grounds. Members of his family lived there until 1968 when the property was abandoned. Later the land was bought by the city of Durham, who reconstructed the West Point Mill, now on the National Register of Historic Places.

Before or after your hike, consider touring the grounds and historic buildings. Some of them are open during certain hours, and the Mangum House can be rented for events. Call ahead for dates and times if you are interested in touring the buildings. Your tour of the park will be interesting as well.

First follow the Laurel Cliff Trail toward the river but then take a spur over to the Buffalo Trail. From there, rock-hop Warren Creek to visit the deep waters of the Sennett Hole on the Eno. Backtrack to climb a bluff above the Eno River, gaining excellent views. The trail drops back down along the water, and you pass the old milldam then come to West Point Mill itself. A short road walk takes you back to your parking spot. Be apprised that user-created paths may take you off the correct route, but all official trails are blazed.

Miles and Directions

0.0 From the park picnic shelter and restrooms, join the Laurel Cliff Trail westerly. Immediately bridge a small branch then climb into woods.

0.1 Head left on the Buffalo Spur leading toward the Buffalo Trail.

0.2 Pass a second intersection and stay straight, as an unnamed trail leaves right.

0.3 Meet the Buffalo Trail. Head right, joining an eroded old roadbed. Rise through hardwoods. Note the parallel track, an even older abandoned, eroded road. Top out in rocky woods.

0.6 Intersect the South River Trail just before reaching Warren Creek. For now, keep straight, rock-hopping Warren Creek on laid stepping-stones, joining the Sennett Hole Trail. Avoid the user-created path running along a sewer line right-of-way. Head into bottomlands stretching toward the Eno River. Reach a rope swing and popular fishing spot in this huge, still hole below a rapid. Backtrack to Warren Creek and the South River Trail.

0.8 Join the South River Trail and walk at first along Warren Creek, then climb a bluff overlooking the confluence of Warren Creek and the Eno River. Here laurel-clad rock bluffs make a scenic setting, especially where rock outcrops allow views of the water below.

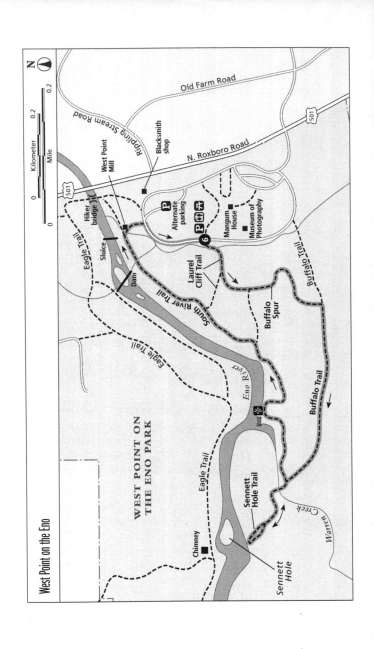

West Point on the Eno

Old Farm Road

Rippling Stream Road

501

N. Roxboro Road

Blacksmith shop

West Point Mill

Alternate parking

Mangum House

Museum of Photography

6

Laurel Cliff Trail

Buffalo Spur

Buffalo Trail

Buffalo Trail

Hiker bridge

Sluice

Dam

Eagle Trail

South River Trail

WEST POINT ON
THE ENO PARK

Eno River

Eagle Trail

Eagle Trail

Sennett Hole Trail

Sennett Hole

Chimney

Warren Creek

N

Kilometer
0.2   0.2

0   Mile

1.0 Come to a view and contemplation bench. Descend from the cliffs.

1.1 Reach the water's edge. A marked nature trail enters on the right. Keep straight on the South River Trail, climbing. User-created trails split left toward bluffs in this potentially confusing area. Just keep the river to your left and you will be fine.

1.2 The other end of the Laurel Cliff Trail comes in on your right. Descend to the river again, with the final part using wood steps.

1.3 Pass a concrete dam on the Eno. Just ahead stands the West Point Mill. Note the dug sluice diverting water to the mill wheel. After reaching the mill, join the park road and follow it back toward the trailhead.

1.5 Return to the picnic shelter and trailhead parking, completing the hike.

7 Shepherd Nature Trail

This is an opportunity to learn about the landscape of the Piedmont while stretching your legs. Set in the Durham Division of the Duke Forest, this loop explores a stream cutting through a swath of undeveloped woods, despite urbanization all around it. The walk, great for kids of all ages, is dotted with interpretive signage and information about the natural world. The Shepherd Nature Trail is your learning conduit. It ends near a picnic shelter ideal for outdoor dining. Next, join a doubletrack path as it rolls through small watersheds divided by hills, making your way back to the trailhead.

Distance: 1.9-mile loop
Hiking time: 1.0–1.5 hours
Difficulty: Easy
Trail surface: Gravel and natural surface
Best season: Year-round
Other trail users: None
Canine compatibility: Leashed dogs permitted

Fees and permits: None
Schedule: Sunrise to sunset
Maps: Duke Forest Durham Division; USGS Northwest Durham
Trail contacts: Office of the Duke Forest, Duke University, PO Box 90332, Durham, NC 27708, (919) 613-8013, www.dukeforest.duke.edu

Finding the trailhead: From exit 107, Duke University West Campus, on US 15/US 501 northeast of Chapel Hill and southwest of downtown Durham, head west on NC 751 and follow it 1.3 miles to Duke Forest and Gate C. Gate 7 is across the road. There is shoulder parking along both gates. Do not block the gates. Trailhead GPS: N36 0.723', W78 58.432'

The Hike

Periodically, hurricanes and tropical storms make their way from the Atlantic Ocean into the Piedmont of central North Carolina. The rain and wind can cause serious damage and devastation. Such was the case when Hurricane Fran in 1989 bulled her way into the greater Triangle, wreaking havoc not only in places like Duke Forest but in urban areas as well. While cleaning up and salvage logging the divisions of Duke Forest, someone came up with the idea to build a nature trail detailing the effects and subsequent results of Hurricane Fran on the forest at large.

Thus the Shepherd Nature Trail came to be. In 2017, the interpretive signage on the Shepherd Nature Trail was replaced and improved, keeping the natural history information imparted along this trail relevant. Learn about the trees and ecology of the forest too.

The smallish stream along which Shepherd Nature Trail travels is perfect for little kids to play in, to flip over a rock and maybe find a salamander, or to spot minnows or crayfish, gaining a greater understanding of the interplay between land and water. There is also a historical component; you will see evidence of past farming as well as a rocked-in spring from the days when water was not accessed through a network of lines spreading underground throughout the Triangle. The Independence Tree is also a fascinating exhibit. Here a tree blown down during Hurricane Fran was cut crossways and its tree rings displayed to show the time periods through which it lived. The name of the tree derives from when it first rose in these forests.

The end of the Shepherd Nature Trail leads to a fine picnic shelter, shaded from the elements, with tables and a fireplace, set far enough back in the woods to be away from the road but not so far that toting picnic supplies would be excessively laborious. Consider adding a picnic to your walk.

You can cut your hike short, just walking the Shepherd Nature Trail, but I recommend adding a secondary loop using the gated forest roads used by Duke Forest personnel to manage the forest. The walking is easy as you undulate over wooded hills, dropping into and climbing out of shallow drainages of intermittent streams. It all adds up to a pleasant woodland stroll, though the secondary loop does require crossing NC 751, a two-lane road with moderate traffic.

Miles and Directions

0.0 Leave north from Gate C on a doubletrack gated gravel road. Curve right to find a stone grill and picnic table. Split left on the singletrack Shepherd Nature Trail. Descend along a fence erected to prevent shortcutting switchbacks. Come to the first of many interpretive signs that are stretched all along the Shepherd Nature Trail.

0.1 Cross a stream on a wooden bridge. This unnamed, clear waterway flows into unpleasantly named Mud Creek. Rise to a hill, passing an old farmer's woodlot. Descend.

0.4 Cross the unnamed stream a second time by bridge. Look for the rocked-in spring just after the creek crossing. Even though this is a perennial stream, farmers knew that most free-flowing streams were contaminated and got their drinking water from springs like this when possible.

0.5 Reach a four-way intersection. Here a forest road goes sharply left. Stay straight, south, on a doubletrack path heading toward Gate 5. Ahead, split right on singletrack, back on the Shepherd Nature Trail in pines and oaks. Enjoy more interpretive signage.

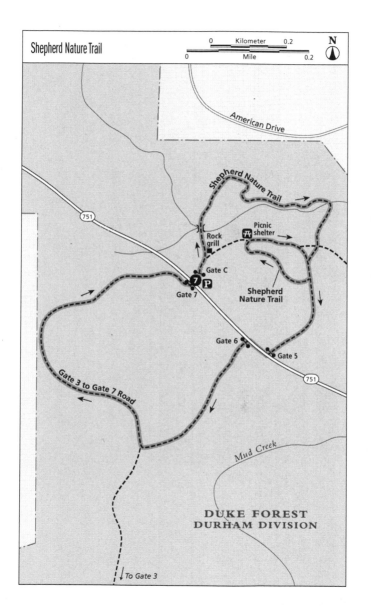

Shepherd Nature Trail

American Drive

751

Shepherd Nature Trail

Rock grill

Picnic shelter

Gate C

7 P

Gate 7

Shepherd Nature Trail

Gate 6

Gate 5

751

Gate 3 to Gate 7 Road

Mud Creek

DUKE FOREST
DURHAM DIVISION

To Gate 3

N

0   Kilometer   0.2
0   Mile   0.2

0.7 The Shepherd Nature Trail ends. Come to a doubletrack. Leave right, passing the picnic shelter on your left. Ahead, split right, again heading toward Gate 5 underneath pines and oaks.

1.0 Reach Gate 5 and NC 751. Turn right and briefly walk along the road to meet Gate 6. Cross the road and pass around Gate 6. Undulate through shallow drainages.

1.3 Turn right at an intersection onto Gate 3 to Gate 7 Road. Curve near a neighborhood.

1.9 Come to Gate 7 and NC 751, completing the walk.

8 Piney Mountain Hike

This hike explores the highs and lows of the Duke Forest's Korstian Division. Start your hike on the Piney Mountain Road to reach the crest of Piney Mountain, standing 200 feet above New Hope Creek below. Drop to the water's edge and squeeze past rocky bluffs. The trail then crosses Piney Mountain Creek and pinches past still more bluffs before opening to richly forested bottomland. Downstream, find sheer bluffs across the water and two milldams. Your return route wanders woods before returning to New Hope Creek and a backtrack. Finally, climb back to the top of Piney Mountain and onto the trailhead.

Distance: 3.8-mile balloon double loop

Hiking time: 2.5–3.5 hours

Difficulty: More challenging in sections

Trail surface: Gravel and natural surface

Best season: Spring for wildflowers and aquatic scenes

Other trail users: None

Canine compatibility: Leashed dogs permitted

Fees and permits: None

Schedule: Sunrise to sunset

Maps: Duke Forest Korstian Division; USGS Chapel Hill

Trail contacts: Office of the Duke Forest, Duke University, PO Box 90332, Durham, NC 27708, (919) 613-8013, www.dukeforest .duke.edu

Finding the trailhead: From exit 270 on I-40, east of Chapel Hill, take US 15/US 501 north toward Duke/Durham. Drive 0.5 mile then turn left on Mount Moriah Road. Drive 1.4 miles then turn right on Erwin Road. Follow Erwin Road for 1.2 miles then turn left on Kerley Road. Follow Kerley Road for 0.2 mile then turn left on Mount Sinai Road and follow it for 0.9 mile to Gate 21 on your left, across the street from Mount Sinai Baptist Church. There is road shoulder parking just past the church. Do not park in the church lot. Trailhead GPS: N35 59.693', W79 0.516'

The Hike

Yes, there are some named mountains in the Piedmont. However, it takes more than a name for a mountain to be a mountain. It also takes a little elevation, and Piney Mountain has that. Rising to an elevation of 452 proud feet above sea level, Piney Mountain stands on the edge of a gorge overlooking New Hope Creek nearly 200 declivitous feet below. And when you stand on the edge of Piney Mountain, it seems a long way down.

The hike starts on a ridgeline stretching south from Mount Sinai Road. A doubletrack leads to the crest of Piney Mountain, where you can look down into the abyss of New Hope Creek. Luckily, foot trails link to New Hope Creek, allowing a sane descent. The hike then squeezes downstream between Pine Mountain and New Hope Creek, where you will be dancing over rocks and between leaning trees bent from previous flooding.

By the way, do not take this hike during high water conditions, as this section of trail might be inundated. The nearest streamflow monitoring gauge is New Hope Creek at Blands, North Carolina. The gauge is located where New Hope Creek flows under the Stagecoach Road Bridge. Though the gauge is downstream of this hike, check this gauge to see if New Hope Creek is flowing at normal levels for any given time. If it is near normal, then you should have no problem getting down the trail. This part of the hike really does squeeze over rocks and even around a couple of outcrops penetrating into the stream.

Next comes the unbridged crossing of Piney Mountain Creek. Again, this should be no problem under normal flows, and even at higher flows you can simply take off your shoes and ford the stream. From there the hike squeezes past a couple more rocky bluff areas bordered by rapids, all making for a scenic albeit more challenging trail. Then the path opens onto richly wooded bottoms and the going is easy, for the steep, rough bluffs are now on the other side of the creek. Look for overhangs amid the rock. Pass an old milldam backed against a bluff, known as the Breached Dam Mill.

Just when you've had all the waterside walking you can stand, the hike comes near Erwin Road and a gristmill site known as the Mann Patterson Mill. The dam and millrace are evident here. After checking this out, cut through woods on Mrs. Browns Trail. Squeeze back upstream on New Hope Creek. Finally, it is time to climb Piney Mountain. After your ascent you may think it really does deserve to be called a mountain.

Miles and Directions

0.0 Head south from Gate 21 on gravel Piney Mountain Road, bordered by pines.

0.5 Reach the top of Piney Mountain and a trail junction. The drop-off is evident to the south. Leave right on a stony footpath. Descend sharply to flats with rock piles from former fields. Come alongside a tributary of New Hope Creek under tulip and sycamore trees. Watch for a stone fence.

0.8 Meet the New Hope Creek North Trail. Head left, downstream, paralleling the rocky, rooty water's edge.

0.9 Squeeze over a sloped, ferny, mossy bluff reaching toward the waters. The stream bends and slows in a pool.

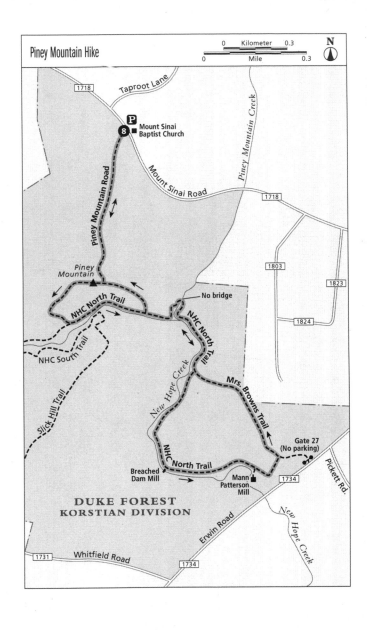

Piney Mountain Hike

0 Kilometer 0.3
0 Mile 0.3

N

1718
Taproot Lane

P
8
Mount Sinai
Baptist Church

Piney Mountain Creek

Mount Sinai Road

Piney Mountain Road

1718

1803

1823

Piney
Mountain

NHC North Trail

No bridge

NHC North Trail

1824

NHC South Trail

Mrs. Browns Trail

New Hope Creek

Slick Hill Trail

NHC North Trail

Gate 27
(No parking)

Pickett Rd.

Breached
Dam Mill

Mann
Patterson
Mill

1734

DUKE FOREST
KORSTIAN DIVISION

New Hope Creek

1731

Whitfield Road

Erwin Road

1734

1.1 Pass the other end of the Piney Mountain Trail. Keep along New Hope Creek then turn up Piney Mountain Creek.

1.2 Cross Piney Mountain Creek. Turn downstream then keep downstream along New Hope Creek.

1.4 Work around a prominent outcrop overlooking the creek.

1.6 Pass Mrs. Browns Trail, your return route. Stay along New Hope Creek.

1.8 View a sheer rock bluff across the creek.

1.9 Walk in view of a partial milldam stretching across the creek, Breached Dam Mill. Overhanging bluffs rise across the water. Cross a big flat.

2.1 The spur to the Mann Patterson Mill leaves right. The loop soon turns left, away from the creek.

2.2 Turn left at Mrs. Browns Trail. It is a short distance right to Gate 27 on Erwin Road. Roll through woods.

2.6 Return to New Hope Creek; backtrack.

3.1 Join new trail, leaving right to climb Piney Mountain.

3.3 Crest out on Piney Mountain. Backtrack on Piney Mountain Road.

3.8 Return to the trailhead, completing the hike.

⑨ Rhododendron Bluff Circuit

This loop visits one of the deepest valleys in the Triangle area. You might even call this part of New Hope Creek a mini gorge as it cuts a rocky, rapid-filled swath beneath Piney Mountain. Situated in the Korstian Division of Duke Forest, upland fire roads lead down to New Hope Creek, where you then join the New Hope Creek South Trail. Enjoy hiking along the rugged and stony stream with bordering rocky flats that resemble waterways of the Carolina mountains. Come upon the base of Rhododendron Bluff, a steep, evergreen-cloaked hill and sheer cliff towering over New Hope Creek. Leave the creek, using forest roads and trails to complete the loop.

Distance: 3.1-mile balloon loop
Hiking time: 2.0–2.5 hours
Difficulty: Moderate, more challenging in sections
Trail surface: Gravel and natural surface
Best season: Year-round
Other trail users: None
Canine compatibility: Leashed dogs permitted

Fees and permits: None
Schedule: Sunrise to sunset
Maps: Duke Forest Korstian Division; USGS Chapel Hill
Trail contacts: Office of the Duke Forest, Duke University, PO Box 90332, Durham, NC 27708, (919) 613-8013, www.duke forest.duke.edu

Finding the trailhead: From exit 270 on I-40, east of Chapel Hill, take US 15/US 501 north toward Duke/Durham. Drive 0.5 mile then turn left on Mount Moriah Road. Drive 1.4 miles then turn right on Erwin Road. Follow Erwin Road 0.5 mile then turn left on Whitfield Road. Follow Whitfield Road for 0.6 mile to Gate 26, on your right.

There is road shoulder parking where designated only. Trailhead GPS: N35 58.670', W79 0.988'

The Hike

Despite the fact that hiking in the various divisions of Duke Forest is not highly touted or advertised in any way, Triangle area hikers seem to make their way to the trails open to the public. The Korstian Division of Duke Forest contains within it arguably the most exhilarating gorge in the area, and thus is one of the more popular parcels of Duke Forest. Although using the word gorge may be a stretch, New Hope Creek has cut a valley that drops off 150 feet from its hilltops in places. This vertical variety adds biodiversity to the watershed, especially when you consider that the winding stream creates multiple exposures, resulting in bluffs where Catawba rhododendron colors the hillsides, and in other places microclimates where wildflowers thrive. Additionally, the large amount of exposed rock enhances the hilly terrain and recalls the rocky Appalachians in the western part of North Carolina.

Make no mistake, the amount of rock, while geologically alluring, adds a challenging element to the hike in some places. The footbed can be very irregular for these parts. However, the walk starts out innocuously enough, tracing gated doubletrack forest roads (closed to the public) through upland oak forests. After dropping off Slick Hill, the hike reaches noisy New Hope Creek, with a concentration of rocky rapids within the Korstian Division that also recalls the mountains. Over the approximately 5-mile stretch between Turkey Farm Road at the west end of Korstian and Erwin Road on the east end, New Hope Creek drops 20 feet per mile, with some stretches approaching 40 feet per mile!

Piney Mountain rises just across from your meeting point with New Hope Creek. Then you turn upstream, working your way over periodically inundated flats as well as stone-pocked slopes. The trail also cuts across sporadic intermittent streambeds. Views of the creek are nearly constant and reveal an everywhere-you-look beauty.

The streamside trekking culminates in the stretch underneath Rhododendron Bluff. Here the sheer rock wall bordered with the lesser-seen evergreen combined with the challenging walking among boulders make for a true highlight. You can also walk up to the top of Rhododendron Bluff to gain a view up New Hope Creek. Enjoy more intimate streamside trekking until you gratefully emerge onto Concrete Bridge Road. The walking is easy now as this doubletrack leads you up and away from New Hope Creek.

Next, a foot trail winds through a restored pine/wiregrass forest that once covered much of the Piedmont but is seldom seen today. Here you can see the lay of the land mostly covered in high grasses and brush mixed with sporadic tall pines. Then, enjoy a final bit of easy trail through oaks to complete the hike.

Miles and Directions

0.0 Head north from Gate 26 on gravel Laurel Hill Road under Piedmont pine/oak woods.

0.2 Split right with Slick Hill Trail, a doubletrack path. Descend northeasterly.

0.7 Reach an auto turnaround. The path morphs to singletrack.

0.9 Meet the New Hope Creek South Trail. Stay right, making a little loop before turning west and heading upstream along New Hope Creek, making quite a splash as it flows.

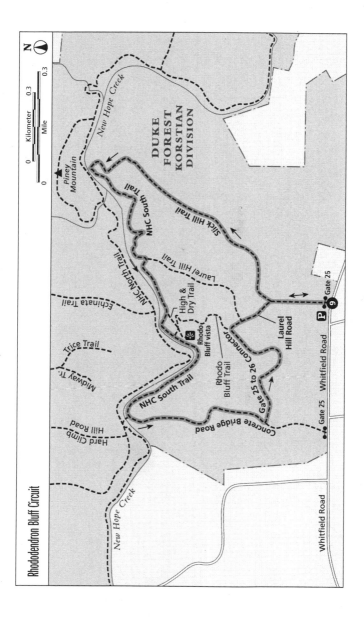

Rhododendron Bluff Circuit

DUKE FOREST KORSTIAN DIVISION

New Hope Creek

Piney Mountain

NHC South Trail

Slick Hill Trail

Laurel Hill Trail

NHC North Trail

Echinata Trail

Trice Trail

Midway Tr.

High & Dry Trail

Rhodo Bluff vista

Rhodo Bluff Trail

Gate 25 to 26 Connector

NHC South Trail

Hard Climb Hill Road

New Hope Creek

Concrete Bridge Road

Laurel Hill Road

Gate 25

Gate 25

Whitfield Road

Whitfield Road

P

9

N

0   0.3 Kilometer
0   0.3 Mile

1.2 Come near an island in the stream. Keep west, bridging intermittent streambeds flowing into New Hope Creek.

1.3 Keep straight after intersecting the Laurel Hill Trail.

1.4 Reach a prominent outcrop overlooking the creek.

1.5 Meet the High & Dry Trail. Stay straight on the New Hope Creek South Trail.

1.6 Keep straight as the Creek Connector heads left. However, if you want a bluff-top view, take the Creek Connector to the Rhodo Bluff Spur to the view. This hike stays along the creek on the New Hope Creek South Trail. Work upstream amid boulders and over outcrops, directly beside the stream, below hemlock and rhododendron.

1.7 Step over an unnamed creek. Continue up the New Hope Creek valley in a rocky, wooded floodplain. Pass an old stone fence from long-ago farming days.

1.9 Reach the fork at Concrete Bridge Road. Turn left on double-track, climbing.

2.4 Turn left on the Gate 25 to Gate 26 Connector. Enter a restored pine/wiregrass ecosystem. Cross two drainages.

2.8 Head right on Laurel Hill Road. Ahead, the Laurel Hill Trail comes in on your left.

2.9 Reach a hilltop and the Slick Hill Trail. Keep right, now backtracking.

3.1 Return to the trailhead, completing the hike.

10 Big Bend Loop

Enjoy a mix of streamside and hilltop hiking on this circuit hike at the Korstian Division of Duke Forest, as well as viewing different forest management practices within the forest. The hike leaves Mount Sinai Road, using forest roads to reach the Wooden Bridge. Here you turn downstream along New Hope Creek. Discover bluffs, bottomlands, and big woods while curving along the creek, including the Big Bend. Leave the stream to climb back to upland woods via wide double-track trail. (**Note:** A couple of sections involve a modicum of scrambling along rock outcrops.)

Distance: 3.7-mile balloon loop
Hiking time: 2.5–3.5 hours
Difficulty: More challenging in short sections
Trail surface: Gravel and natural surface
Best season: Spring for wildflowers and aquatic scenes
Other trail users: None
Canine compatibility: Leashed dogs permitted

Fees and permits: None
Schedule: Sunrise to sunset
Maps: Duke Forest Korstian Division; USGS Chapel Hill
Trail contacts: Office of the Duke Forest, Duke University, PO Box 90332, Durham, NC 27708, (919) 613-8013, www.dukeforest .duke.edu

Finding the trailhead: From exit 270 on I-40, east of Chapel Hill, take US 15/US 501 north toward Duke/Durham. Drive 0.5 mile then turn left on Mount Moriah Road. Drive 1.4 miles then turn right on Erwin Road. Follow Erwin Road for 1.2 miles then turn left on Kerley Road. Follow Kerley Road for 0.2 mile then turn left on Mount Sinai Road and follow it for 1.8 miles to Gate 23 on your left. There is limited parking in a lot beside Gate 23. Do not block the gate or park illegally along Mount Sinai Road. Trailhead GPS: N35 59.971', W79 1.430'

The Hike

A perusal of topographic maps of the Triangle area reveals the Eno River and New Hope Creek to have the steepest valleys in the region. While the hills of the Eno River may be a little higher, the bluffs along New Hope Creek within the Korstian Division of Duke Forest are impressive nonetheless, rising in wild isolation from rocky banks to wooded heights nearly 200 feet high. The combination of deep valleys and nature aplenty adds up to a surprisingly wild experience within easy reach of Chapel Hill and Durham residents.

And this particular hike travels the longest stretch of steep gorge along New Hope Creek. You first start out innocuously along Concrete Bridge Road (vehicle access only to Duke Forest personnel), heading south before working your way to Wooden Bridge Road. Along the route, you pass by differing stands of pines and hardwoods managed by Duke University. Signs in front of these tree stands reveal particular forestry management practices and what year each stand underwent these practices, such as prescribed burning, thinning, partial harvesting, hardwood removal, and more. This allows visitors to observe the different effects from varied forestry management techniques. You will see tree stands of differing ages, from youngish pine plantations to mature tree stands to now-timbered-over areas, and the process of regeneration.

After learning a little bit about forestry, drop to New Hope Creek at the Wooden Bridge, a road span over the creek that also serves as a site marker within the forest. Nearby you will find an old millstone from the days when power-generating mills stretched all along New Hope Creek. From here the New Hope Creek North Trail is your conduit for heading deeper into the valley, bordered by bottomlands in some areas and steep bluffs in others. Sometimes you will be walking in a bottomland and gazing across at bluffs. In other places you will be navigating over rocky prominences extending directly into the creek, with more rocky terrain rising above you.

After making one sharp curve you reach the Big Bend, a curve where the stream goes from due west to due east. In most places you hike along the water's edge; in others the trail works through wooded and irregular floodplain. Upon reaching the ford at Concrete Bridge Road, you will appreciate the easy walking afforded by the road, a gravel doubletrack. Rise from the waterway, passing more managed timber stands. Make your way almost due north, completing the loop and returning to the trailhead.

Miles and Directions

0.0   Head southwest from Gate 23 on gravel and mostly level Concrete Bridge Road, shaded by tall pines and oaks.

0.3   Reach an intersection near a USGS well-monitoring station. Turn right here on an unnamed doubletrack. Head west, flanked by tightly grown pine stands.

0.5   Come to another intersection. Head left on Wooden Bridge Road, making a gradual descent toward New Hope Creek, with youngish forest on your right.

1.0   Reach the Wooden Bridge just after passing a millstone on your right. Leave left on the New Hope Creek North Trail. Enter riverside flats of beech and ironwood on a singletrack foot trail. Gravel bars, rocky shoals, and bluffs are elements of stream scenes. Cross rocky sections and intermittent drainages.

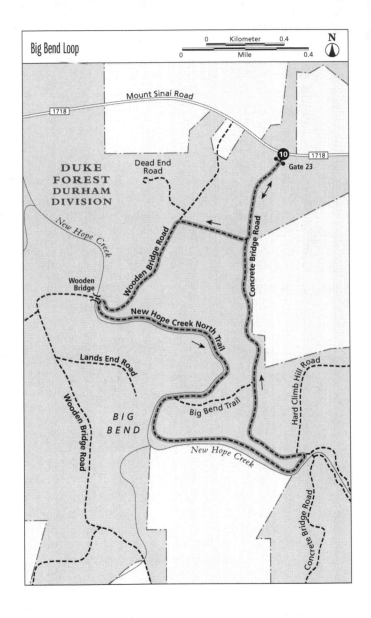

Big Bend Loop

0   Kilometer   0.4

0   Mile   0.4

N

1718   Mount Sinai Road

DUKE
FOREST
DURHAM
DIVISION

Dead End
Road

10   1718
Gate 23

New Hope Creek

Wooden
Bridge

Wooden Bridge Road

Concrete Bridge Road

New Hope Creek North Trail

Lands End Road

Wooden Bridge Road

BIG
BEND

Big Bend Trail

Hard Climb Hill Road

New Hope Creek

Concrete Bridge Road

1.5 Pass a huge tulip tree on trail left. Just ahead, the path curves right and squeezes past a bluff and the stream. You may have to briefly use hands and feet in this short segment.

1.7 Stay straight as the Big Bend Trail comes in on your left. The walking is easy while curving around the inside of the Big Bend. A long rapid flows through the Big Bend.

2.2 Another bluff rises on the north side of New Hope Creek, forcing hikers to navigate a slope above an outcrop jutting into New Hope Creek.

2.5 Come to Concrete Bridge Road and the concrete ford across New Hope Creek. Head left, ascending on Concrete Bridge Road. Just ahead, pass Hard Climb Hill Road on your right. Keep ascending.

2.9 Meet the other end of the Big Bend Trail after passing by a timbered clearing. Keep straight on Concrete Bridge Road. Pass near the forest boundary and houses.

3.4 Complete the loop portion of the hike at a three-way intersection. Keep straight.

3.7 Return to the trailhead, completing the hike.

11 Johnston Mill Nature Preserve

This hike explores a protected parcel of the upper New Hope Creek watershed. Follow New Hope Creek downstream past two former mill sites, then make a loop around a tributary—Old Field Creek—walking hilly bluffs and streamside flats. These watercourses deliver beauty in each season, luring you to return for multiple visits.

Distance: 3.5-mile balloon loop
Hiking time: 1.5–2.5 hours
Difficulty: Moderate
Trail surface: Natural;
Best season: Spring for wildflowers
Other trail users: None
Canine compatibility: Leashed dogs permitted

Fees and permits: None
Schedule: Sunrise to sunset
Maps: Johnston Mill Nature Preserve Trail Map; USGS Chapel Hill
Trail contacts: Triangle Land Conservancy, 514 South Duke St., Durham, NC 27701, (919) 908-8809, www.triangleland.org

Finding the trailhead: From exit 266 on I-40, north of Chapel Hill, take NC 86 north for 1.8 miles to turn right on Mount Sinai Road. Follow it for 1.1 miles to the parking area on the right just before the bridge over New Hope Creek. Trailhead GPS: N35 59.730', W79 3.249'

The Hike

Johnston Mill Nature Preserve comes in at 296 acres, and protects a segment of New Hope Creek in Orange County. New Hope Creek cuts steep bluffs as it meanders through hills then curves south, carving a valley dividing Chapel Hill from Durham. It becomes dammed upon entering Chatham County, as the waters of Jordan Lake flood the lowermost

New Hope Creek valley. It is in this lake that New Hope Creek meets its mother stream, the Haw River.

Since New Hope Creek is deep in the Triangle, it has been under continuous development pressure, making this preserve even more valuable. This pressure was recognized by the North Carolina Natural Heritage Program as well as being "one of Orange County's most important natural areas." Fortunately for local hikers and nature enthusiasts, the Triangle Land Conservancy purchased and protected this and several other such preserves.

The 296 acres that comprise Johnston Mill Nature Preserve were bought in the late 1990s for over 3 million dollars. Imagine how much this land would cost today! Consider that when you enjoy this conserved tract. The hike leaves the Mount Sinai trailhead and immediately drops to meet New Hope Creek. Follow the perennial waterway downstream as it bends in nearly continuous arcs, showing gravel bars in summer and fall when flowing low, but also sporting evidence of winter floods—downstream bent tree trunks, logs piled against rocks, brush hanging in trees. With increased urbanization, having a natural floodplain helps absorb fast runoff from asphalt roads and parking lots. The trail clambers around rock outcrops. Ahead you will see scattered stone remains of a gristmill located across the creek in Hogans Bottom. Look for remnant rock walls and the old tailrace. Continue following New Hope Creek downstream to reach its confluence with Old Field Creek. The New Hope Creek valley has been cultivated for centuries, logged, too. Old Field Creek likely got its name from its bottomland being cultivated. The land has since healed from its time with the plow and the axe.

Before heading that way, our hike continues down New Hope Creek as it makes a dramatic bend. We reach the site of Johnston Mill. A portion of the milldam is still intact and easily visible. The hike then heads to Old Field Creek. Here, you wander through a stand of impressive gray beech trees on a bluff above Old Field Creek. Stay above the stream in rich woods, then turn up smaller Johnston Branch.

The hike bridges Johnston Branch then spans Old Field Creek, comfortably ensconced in woods, completely belying its name. The Old Field Bluff Trail meanders through bucolic rolling woods, a perfect place to soak in fall color. Finally, you return to New Hope Creek, backtracking to the trailhead.

Miles and Directions

0.0 From the parking area off Mount Sinai Road, join the single-track Robins Trail. Drop off a rise, bisect a flat, and shortly come upon New Hope Creek. Turn right, downstream. New Hope Creek alternates in singing shoals and lazy pools. Tall hardwoods rise in the ferny floodplain.

0.2 The trail comes to a bluff. Take the wooden steps right, ascending above the sheer rock outcrop.

0.3 Pass under a powerline. Note the rugged rock formations below, through which New Hope Creek flows. Just ahead, reach a trail intersection. Here, the Bluebird Trail leaves right, and roughly follows the powerline clearing. Stay straight with the Robins Trail, hiking under tall tulip trees.

0.4 Pass beside an old unnamed mill site. It almost looks like a rapid, with lots of stones strewn into the creek. Look for remnants of the old tailrace.

0.6 Come to an intersection. Here, the Old Field Bluff Trail leaves right. This will be your return route. For now, stay straight and immediately span Old Field Creek on a bridge, then come to a four-way trail intersection with the Beech Loop. Here, stay left with the Robins Trail toward Johnston Mill. Course through richly vegetated flats that will be alive with wildflowers in spring.

0.7 Bridge Booth Branch very near Turkey Farm Road. The trail then squeezes between Turkey Farm Road and New Hope Creek.

0.8 Reach the old Johnston Mill site. Drop to New Hope Creek. Look upstream at the remains of the milldam. Imagine the activity that went on here, the locals gathering to visit and swap stories, then imagine the flood that took away the mill. Robins Trail continues curving through bottoms, but we backtrack toward the Beech Loop.

1.0 Return to the four-way intersection and the Beech Loop. Stay straight here. Come directly alongside Old Field Creek. This is another favorable wildflower area. Look for twisted hornbeam trees in the flats. Rise above the river and enter a stand of mature, gray trunked beech trees on this northwest facing slope.

1.2 Meet the other end of the Beech Loop. Stay straight here, joining the Old Field Bluff Trail. Turn in and out of small hollows with boardwalk bridges amid more regal beeches.

1.5 Reach the Creekwood Spur. This leads left to a neighborhood. Stay right here, still on the Old Field Bluff Trail. Climb well above the creek, at the top end of a steep slope.

1.9 Drop to Johnston Branch, to cross it on a bridge. Descend toward Old Field Creek.

2.0 Bridge Old Field Creek, then climb into hilly woods.

2.2 Open onto a mown meadow. Next, turn left, passing under a powerline. Reenter woods.

2.4 Bridge an intermittent tributary.

2.5 Reach the powerline again. Head left, following the powerline about 50 yards. Here, the Bluebird Trail keeps straight under the powerline but we turn right reentering woods on the Old Field Bluff Trail.

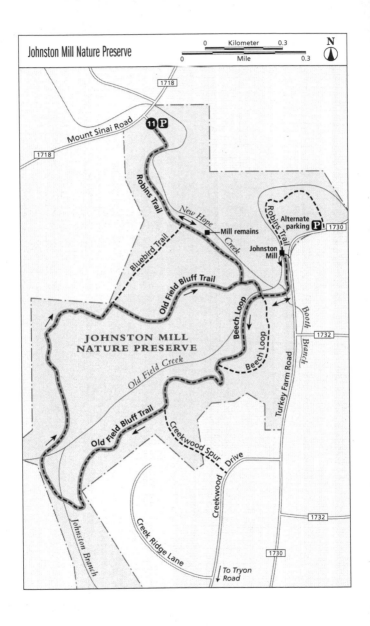

Johnston Mill Nature Preserve

Kilometer
0   0.3
Mile
0   0.3

N

1718

Mount Sinai Road

11 P

1718

Robins Trail

New Hope

Mill remains

Creek

Robins Trail

Alternate parking

P 1730

Johnston Mill

Bluebird Trail

Old Field Bluff Trail

Beech Loop

Beech Loop

JOHNSTON MILL NATURE PRESERVE

Old Field Creek

Booth Branch

Turkey Farm Road

1732

Old Field Bluff Trail

Creekwood Spur

Creekwood Drive

1732

Johnston Branch

Creek Ridge Lane

To Tryon Road

1730

2.9 Reach a trail intersection after descending through woods. Here, you turn left on Robins Trail and backtrack.

3.5 Return to the Mount Sinai Road trailhead, finishing the hike.

12 Cedar Falls Park

This park nestled in the town of Chapel Hill contains some surprisingly hilly and scenic terrain—and its namesake Cedar Falls. You will wend your way through a potentially confusing but fun network of nature trails, leaving the main park area for Cedar Falls, easily heard before seen if Cedar Fork is flowing boldly. From there you wind to the southern end of the wooded park, then stroll north in hills back to the trailhead.

Distance: 1.3-mile balloon double loop

Hiking time: 1.0 hour

Difficulty: Easy

Trail surface: Mostly natural surface

Best season: When local streams are flowing strongly

Other trail users: None

Canine compatibility: Leashed dogs permitted

Fees and permits: None

Schedule: Sunrise to 10 p.m.

Maps: Cedar Falls Park; USGS Chapel Hill

Trail contacts: Cedar Falls Park, 501 Weaver Dairy Rd., Chapel Hill, NC 27514, (919) 968-2784, www.townofchapelhill.org/

Finding the trailhead: From exit 266 on I-40, north of Chapel Hill, go south on NC 86 for 0.5 mile to turn left on Weaver Dairy Road at a traffic light. Follow Weaver Dairy Road east for 1.5 miles; Cedar Falls Park will be on your right. Trailhead GPS: N35 57.574', W79 1.941'

The Hike

Situated in Chapel Hill, 65-acre Cedar Falls Park really does have a waterfall! Okay, so maybe it isn't like those vertical cataracts in the western part of the state, but Cedar Falls sure can make some noise when flowing strongly. Here a portion of Cedar Fork flows into the park boundaries, where it slices through a rock impasse, cutting a short but narrow gorge as it splashes onward to meet Booker Creek, itself a tributary of Little Creek, which then flows into Jordan Lake.

The park is a mixture of ball fields and natural area. The ball fields are concentrated in the upper, northern part of the park along Weaver Dairy Road, while the forested natural parcel of the park comprises the balance of the preserve, which is bordered by residential areas. The former tobacco and cotton farm of Jesse Johnson was purchased by the town of Chapel Hill in 1979 and now serves as a venue for organized sports, including East Chapel Hill High School across the street, as well as a trail-laden getaway for Chapel Hill residents who want a quick escape into nature.

Cedar Fork hasn't had that much distance to flow boldly from its nearby beginning in hills west of the park; therefore its flow is normally mild. However, the stream does cut a steep-sided valley that will surprise hikers who expect less rock and less vertical terrain in the heart of Chapel Hill. Rather than vertical drops the falls are more of a series of fast-moving angled cascades that dash over tan, resistant rock divided by pools. Be careful when you descend to the falls, as the spot is rocky, steep, and sometimes slick. Furthermore, do not continue downstream from the trail access to the falls, since a residence and private property are located there. In fact, the entire park is bordered by residences. Rather than being dismayed by dwellings, instead appreciate a wild preserve being in a sea of civilization.

The hike utilizes an interconnected network of nature trails that has the potential to confuse the hiker due to the sheer number of intersections. However, the trails are color-coded, with maps located at key trail intersections.

Furthermore, the park is too small to get truly lost. Leave the main parking area near the ball fields, passing the restroom, and begin working a counterclockwise loop. Shortly you leave the asphalt trail leading to tennis courts and join a natural surface path in a mixture of hardwoods and pines. The hilly trek turns into the Cedar Fork watershed, where a spur trail dips to Cedar Falls. No matter the water flow, the mini gorge of Cedar Fork makes a craggy, rocky, attractive site. After clambering back up from the falls, you will reach the southerly end of the park and a neighborhood access from Lakeshore Lane. The loop then turns north, where the intertwined pathways will keep you looking at your map. Eventually you make your way back to the trailhead. The upside of all these nature trails is they make possible extending this hike, though you may have to backtrack a bit, or cover some ground twice.

Miles and Directions

0.0   From the restrooms on the west side of the parking area, pick up the asphalt path heading toward the tennis courts. Pass the playground on your right then split right on a natural surface track to meet the Purple Trail. Cut right again and join the Purple/Yellow Trail as it turns south. Wander through hillside forest. Ahead, the Yellow Trail leaves left; stay straight with the Purple Trail.

0.2   A spur trail leaves right, linking to Cedar Fork Trail, a neighborhood road. Keep straight, southbound. Just ahead, the Orange Trail leaves left. Stay with the Purple Trail as it keeps south and drops off a steep hill. Ahead, an unnamed path leaves right and rejoins on the downhill.

0.5   The Red Trail leaves left. Keep straight then split right with the spur dropping to Cedar Falls. If flowing well, you can hear the stream. Descend on a somewhat steep rock and

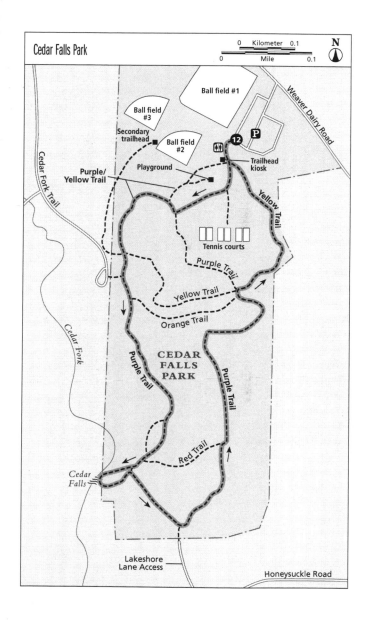

Cedar Falls Park

0 Kilometer 0.1
0 Mile 0.1

N

Weaver Dairy Road

Ball field #1

Ball field #3

Secondary trailhead

Ball field #2

P

12

Trailhead kiosk

Playground

Purple/Yellow Trail

Yellow Trail

Cedar Fork Trail

Tennis courts

Purple Trail

Yellow Trail

Orange Trail

Cedar Fork

CEDAR FALLS PARK

Purple Trail

Purple Trail

Red Trail

Cedar Falls

Lakeshore Lane Access

Honeysuckle Road

dirt path. Drop to Cedar Falls as it makes a multi-tiered slide over rock then continues south out of sight and into private property. Loop back up from the falls, rejoining the Purple Trail.

0.7 Come to the Lakeshore Lane neighborhood access after crossing a boardwalk over a wetland. Stay with the Purple Trail, now heading north. Ahead, pass the intersection with the Red Trail.

1.0 Come to a shortcut linking to the Orange Trail. Head right here, still on the Purple Trail.

1.1 Five pathways come together in a short distance. Leave the Purple Trail and join the Yellow Trail for the longest loop. The park tennis courts are visible through the trees.

1.3 Return to the trailhead, completing the hike.

13 Bolin Creek Trail

This surprisingly attractive greenway takes you on a journey up the Bolin Creek watershed. Start your trek at Community Center Park, with its numerous facilities, then head upstream along Bolin Creek. The trail leads into a hill-bordered vale while passing through occasional wider swaths of protected land along with narrower wooded stretches. Enjoy multiple views of the shoals, gravel bars, and pools of Bolin Creek while on the asphalt path, well integrated into Chapel Hill. Martin Luther King Jr. Boulevard is a good place to turn around, though you can go a mile farther, since the trail was extended in 2019.

Distance: 3.0-mile there-and-back
Hiking time: 1.5–2.0 hours
Difficulty: Easy
Trail surface: Mostly asphalt, some concrete
Best season: Year-round
Other trail users: Bicyclers, joggers

Canine compatibility: Leashed dogs permitted
Fees and permits: None
Schedule: Sunrise to 10 p.m.
Maps: Bolin Creek and Battle Branch Trails; USGS Chapel Hill
Trail contacts: Chapel Hill Community Center, 120 S. Estes Dr., Chapel Hill, NC 27514, (919) 968-2790, www.townofchapelhill.org

Finding the trailhead: From the intersection of US 15/501/Fordham Boulevard and Raleigh Road, east of downtown Chapel Hill, head north on Fordham Boulevard for 1.1 miles to turn left on South Estes Drive. Drive west for 0.4 mile to turn left into Community Center Park. The Bolin Creek Trail starts on the right as you enter the park, before reaching the community center building. Trailhead GPS: N35 55.623', W79 1.923'

The Hike

Bolin Creek is a linear strip of wildness snaking through Chapel Hill. It offers a chance to walk a watershed, a watery ribbon winding through the woods, where hills rise 150 feet from the stream's edge. Luckily for us, this trail harbors not only a wealth of trees that change with the seasons, but the Bolin Creek Valley is also rich in wildflowers, from trout lilies to jack-in-the-pulpits to wild azaleas. Spring is a good time to visit, but so is summertime when the creek forms a hallway of coolness and the stream becomes a fun place for kids' water play. In fall the variety of hardwoods deliver a color cornucopia, putting a smile on a hiker's face. Winter is more barren, but also is the time to view rock outcrops situated along the creek.

Like most greenways around the country, the Bolin Creek Trail is laid out along a stream that was undeveloped along its immediate banks due to flooding and being a right-of-way for local sewage lines. Before the United States was even a country, a settler named Benjamin Bolin farmed this area and lent his name to the creek that ran through his property, much of which is now covered by University Mall, across the street from Community Center Park. Later, other settlers began to populate what became Orange County, named for the King of England, William of Orange. The settlers built gristmills along Bolin Creek, but these sites have mostly been obliterated by time, development, and high water.

Interestingly, one of the University of North Carolina's most famed graduates, Andy Griffith, actually lived in a house overlooking Bolin Creek for a period. Just when he was getting started in his entertainment career, Andy Griffith returned to Chapel Hill after teaching for a year at Goldsboro High School. While living at this house, 1318 Homestead Road, the future television sheriff and lawyer got his first professional contract, and away he went into television history.

Consider such musings while walking the Bolin Creek Trail. Start at Community Center Park, with its ample parking, picnic possibilities, and outdoor art, then head west along Bolin Creek. The way is briefly confusing as you emerge onto a street, Dickerson Court, then leave the road and pass under Franklin Street. The trail then picks up momentum as it passes through a larger park parcel. High wooded hills rise from the gurgling waterway. You will notice that despite the sewage lines being mostly buried underground, access ports are visible. However, these have been painted in muted natural tones that blend into the landscape. Meanwhile the stream twists and turns, slowing in pools and speeding in shoals. Tan sandbars that form on creek bends lure you to investigate. You are never far from houses, but the stream and woods offer plenty of eye appeal. A spur path leads up to Elizabeth Street; however, you cross Bolin Creek by bridge and continue upstream. Step over Bolinwood Drive near the stream's confluence with Mill Race Branch. Keep west, passing through a rich wildflower area. Cross a wetland on an elevated wooden bridge before reaching busy Martin Luther King Jr. Boulevard. From here, the Bolin Creek Trail continues west a mile to Umstead Park.

Miles and Directions

0.0 The Bolin Creek Trail leaves west from Barrett Lane, the entrance road to Community Center Park. Pass through an attractive area landscaped with trees, a gazebo, and outdoor art. Bolin Creek flows to your right. Just ahead, emerge onto

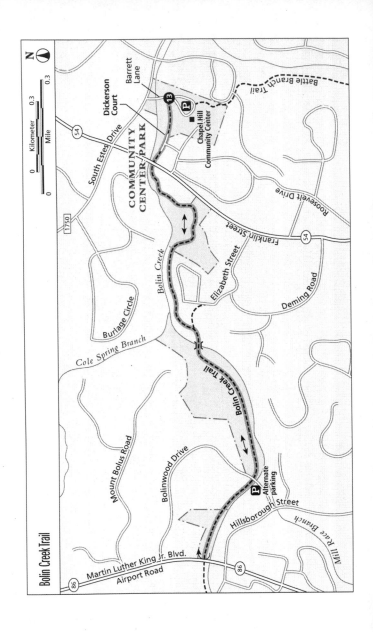

Bolin Creek Trail

N

COMMUNITY
CENTER PARK

Barrett Lane

Dickerson Court

13

Chapel Hill
Community Center

Battle Branch Trail

Roosevelt Drive

South Estes Drive

54

1750

Bolin Creek

Franklin Street

54

Elizabeth Street

Deming Road

Burlage Circle

Cole Spring Branch

Bolin Creek Trail

Mount Bolus Road

Bolinwood Drive

Alternate
parking

Hillsborough Street

Mill Race Branch

Martin Luther King Jr. Blvd.
Airport Road

86

86

0   Kilometer   0.3

0   Mile   0.3

Dickerson Court, a dead-end street. Stay straight along the street, return to greenway, then pass under Franklin Street. (Steps lead up to Franklin Street.) Keep straight on the Bolin Creek Trail as it wanders west.

0.3 Enter a junglesque bottomland. Densely vegetated flats spread to your right while a hill rises sharply to your left. Ahead, the trail comes right alongside Bolin Creek, where you can check out the watercourse up close, especially when accessing one of the many waterside gravel bars.

0.8 A paved spur leads left and uphill to Elizabeth Street. From here the Bolin Creek Trail curves right and bridges Bolin Creek. You are now on the north side of the waterway in another relatively wide swath of parkland. This is a good wildflower area.

1.2 Reach and cross Bolinwood Drive. Note the alternate on-street parking on Bolinwood Drive south of the greenway.

1.5 After rising over a wetland via elevated wooden bridge, reach NC 86/Martin Luther King Jr. Boulevard/Airport Road. Back-track or continue to Umstead Park.

3.0 Return to the trailhead, finishing the hike.

14 Battle Branch Trail

You will enjoy this natural surface greenway that links Chapel Hill's Community Center Park to the University of North Carolina's Battle Park. Leave Community Center Park, cutting through a residential area before joining the Lower Trail along splashy Battle Branch, which you bridge. Turn west, continuing upstream to meet historic Battle Park, with its trail network. Rock outcrops and big hills will surprise most first-time hikers. Your return route uses the Upper Trail, adding variety to the trek.

Distance: 3.2-mile balloon loop
Hiking time: 1.5-2.0 hours
Difficulty: Easy-moderate
Trail surface: Natural
Best season: Year-round
Other trail users: Joggers
Canine compatibility: Leashed dogs permitted
Fees and permits: None

Schedule: Sunrise to 10 p.m.
Maps: Tanyard Branch Trail, Bolin Creek Trail, Battle Branch Trail; USGS Chapel Hill
Trail contacts: Chapel Hill Community Center, 120 S. Estes Dr., Chapel Hill, NC 27514, (919) 968-2790, www.townofchapelhill .org

Finding the trailhead: From the intersection of US 15/501/Fordham Boulevard and Raleigh Road, east of downtown Chapel Hill, head north on Fordham Boulevard for 1.1 miles to turn left on South Estes Drive. Drive west for 0.4 mile to turn left into Community Center Park. The Battle Branch Trail starts on the left as you face the community center building. Trailhead GPS: N35 55.623', W79 1.923'

The Hike

Battle Branch Trail serves as a link between two of Chapel Hill's better parks. Community Center Park is a public facility featuring an indoor swimming pool, climbing wall, and basketball court. Outdoors, the park has a picnic area, playground, and rose garden—and trails too. Not only does the Battle Branch Trail start here, but so does the Bolin Creek Trail, also detailed in this guide. Battle Branch is the more challenging of the two pathways, as it is natural surface and has more vertical variation, plus a few unbridged creek crossings. Before worrying about these creek crossings, know that even they can be avoided.

Battle Park, part of the University of North Carolina (UNC) campus, is known for its historical components. It also has additional footpaths besides the ones used on this hike. Though Battle Branch Trail can be seen as a conduit between the two parks, it is also a worthy walk in its own right. Leave Community Center Park, cutting across a wetland. You briefly follow Willow Drive then turn up Battle Branch on a foot trail. After a spur leaves left to Sugarberry Road, the Battle Branch Trail itself splits into two parallel paths—the Lower Trail and the Upper Trail. The Lower Trail is your outbound route. Here a singletrack footpath dashes between trees and down along Battle Branch, then squeezes past outcrops in bottomland and along slopes, ultimately to reunite with the Upper Trail near a bridged crossing of Battle Branch. The trail widens here, and you pass a spur access to Sandy Creek Trail, a neighborhood road.

The hike then curves west with Battle Branch to where another bridge signifies the entrance to historic Battle Park, named for an early president of the University of North

Carolina. Even though this park is on UNC property, it is open to public access. The trail then crisscrosses Battle Branch without benefit of footbridge (no problem as parallel paths in Battle Park make the crossings avoidable). Visit the old Poplar Picnic Place then rise to reach Park Place and UNC Parking Lot N-3 (alternate weekend and after 5 p.m. weekdays parking on the UNC campus).

Your return route backtracks through Battle Park, but on your way back take the Upper Trail. It is more level and adds new pathway to your hiking experience. The watershed as a whole is heavily wooded, good for wildflowers while Battle Branch sings an outdoorsy tune for your there-and-back.

Miles and Directions

0.0 As you face the front door of the Chapel Hill Community Center, look left for the Battle Branch Trail. It leaves as a natural surface footpath, southbound. Go just a short distance then leave left from Community Center Park on a boardwalk bridge crossing a wetland. Come to Willow Drive. Join the sidewalk and cross Valley Park Drive. Just ahead, the signed Battle Branch Trail leaves right as a footpath and enters rich woods.

0.2 Reach a trail intersection. Here a spur leads left for Sugarberry Road, bridging Battle Branch. Stay straight with the Battle Branch Trail.

0.3 The Battle Branch Trail splits. Stay left with the Lower Trail, a singletrack footpath heading for the University of North Carolina campus. The winding, narrow path comes alongside Battle Branch as it slaloms southward. The Upper Trail runs parallel to the Lower Trail at a higher elevation. Short wooden bridges span braids of Battle Branch and intermittent tributaries. Wood and earth steps help cut down on erosion in hilly spots.

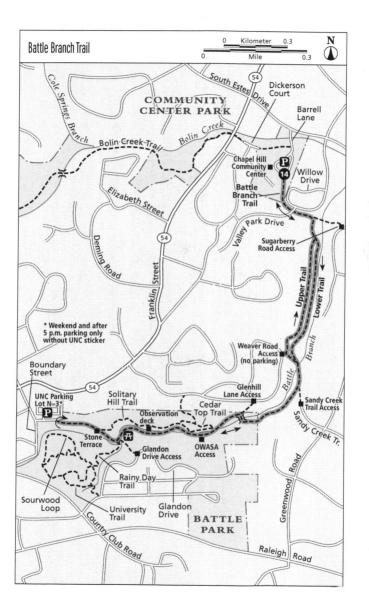

Battle Branch Trail

Kilometer 0
0.3

Mile 0
0.3

N

COMMUNITY
CENTER PARK

South Estes Drive

Dickerson
Court

Barrell
Lane

54

Cole Springs Branch

Bolin-Creek-Trail

Bolin Creek

Chapel Hill
Community
Center

P
14

Willow
Drive

Battle
Branch
Trail

Elizabeth Street

Valley Park Drive

Sugarberry
Road Access

Deming Road

Franklin Street

54

Upper Trail

Lower Trail

Battle Branch

Weaver Road
Access
(no parking)

* Weekend and after
5 p.m. parking only
without UNC sticker

Boundary
Street

54

Solitary
Hill Trail

Glenhill
Lane Access

Sandy
Creek
Trail Access

UNC Parking
Lot N-3*

P

Observation
deck

Cedar
Top Trail

Sandy Creek Tr.

Stone
Terrace

Glandon Drive Access

OWASA
Access

Glandon
Drive

Greenwood Road

Sourwood
Loop

Rainy Day
Trail

University
Trail

Country Club Road

BATTLE
PARK

Raleigh Road

0.4 Quickly bridge Battle Branch twice in succession, working around a bluff. Ironwood, tulip trees, and sweetgum shade the track.

0.6 The Lower Trail and Upper Trail meet just before crossing Battle Branch on a substantial bridge near Weaver Road. Keep south on a wider track.

0.7 The Sandy Creek Trail access leads left. Stay right and curve west, still on Battle Branch Trail.

0.9 Bridge Battle Branch yet again at a trail kiosk. Enter Battle Park and the UNC campus. Climb a hill right and pass the Glenhill Lane Access. Stay left on the main trail of Battle Park, known as OWASA Access (Orange Water and Sewer Authority).

1.1 Come to the nature trail network of Battle Park. Stay with the wider OWASA Access. It begins a series of five creek crossings that are rock hops under normal water levels.

1.3 Pass by the old rock fireplace of the Poplar Picnic Place.

1.4 Stay right at an intersection, bridging Battle Branch and a tributary. Here the Rainy Day Trail and an access to Glandon Drive leave left. Stay right with the OWASA Access. Pass the Stone Terrace and the Solitary Hill Trail, heading uphill.

1.6 Emerge at Park Place and UNC parking lot N-3. Backtrack. On your return trip, take the Upper Trail for new trail and/or some of Battle Park's nature trails.

3.2 Return to Community Center Park, completing the hike.

15 Battle Park

Battle Park, once known as Battle's Woods, may be the oldest hiking destination in the Chapel Hill area. The 93-acre preserve is named for the student and later president of the University of North Carolina, Kemp Plummer Battle, who back in the 1840s laid out trails along the creek that bears his name. Today Battle would be proud to know his woods have been turned into a park with trails enough for a rewarding double loop that explores the streams and hills of this wooded swath of the UNC campus, as well as visits the historic outdoor Forest Theater.

Distance: 2.1-mile balloon double loop
Hiking time: 1.0–1.5 hours
Difficulty: Easy
Trail surface: Natural
Best season: Year-round
Other trail users: Joggers
Canine compatibility: Leashed dogs permitted

Fees and permits: None
Schedule: Sunrise to sunset
Maps: Battle Park Pedestrian Trails; USGS Chapel Hill
Trail contacts: North Carolina Botanical Garden, 100 Old Mason Farm Rd., Chapel Hill, NC 27517, (919) 962-0522, www .ncbg.unc.edu

Finding the trailhead: From exit 273 on I-40, east of Chapel Hill, take Raleigh Road west toward UNC-Chapel Hill. After 3.5 miles turn right onto Country Club Road. In about two blocks, Battle Park and Forest Theater are on the right. There is metered parking on Country Club Road. You can also park at UNC Lot N-3 after 5 p.m. and on weekends without a permit. To access this lot, turn right onto Boundary Street from Country Club Road. Follow it a short distance then take a sharp right onto Park Place; Lot N-3 is on your left. Trailhead GPS: N35 55.623', W79 1.923'

The Hike

Back in the 1840s the University of North Carolina (UNC) was nothing like it is today—in size, scope, or student body. However, it was North Carolina's state institution of higher learning. As it has been a Tar Heel tradition with many families, Kemp Battle attended the university from which his father graduated. His father, Judge William Horn Battle, went so far as to move to Chapel Hill in order for his offspring to attend UNC. By 1849 Kemp Battle had not only completed his studies but was valedictorian of his class. He took to the woods to practice his commencement address. It was then he came to love this natural parcel of Chapel Hill, going so far as to lay out hiking trails and name specific features.

Battle left Chapel Hill for a law career in Raleigh. After the Civil War he was instrumental in getting UNC reopened in 1875, for which he was rewarded with the presidency of UNC. Battle served a fifteen-year stretch as university president, then retired to being a history professor. It was during his tenure as school president that this forest became known as Battle's Woods and the stream that flows through it Battle Branch.

Now surrounded by civilization, what became Battle Park retains much of the charm from the 1800s. While hiking here you can still stop by the Monarch of the Forest, a sizable tulip tree named by Mr. Battle. The hike first uses the OWASA Access (Orange Water and Sewer Authority) to enter the valley of Battle Branch. Stop by the Stone Terrace, where you can look down on gurgling Battle Branch as it courses between remarkably steep hills. From there, turn up a tributary on the Rainy Day Trail then make a loop using the Deer Track Trail and the Sourwood Loop.

Pass by the historic Forest Theater, a stone outdoor entertainment venue built in the early 1900s, then rebuilt in 1940. Today the stone music and acting locale is a UNC icon that is also used for weddings. From there you loop back down to Battle Branch, passing the Poplar Picnic Place, where generations of Chapel Hill residents have enjoyed an outdoor meal. Continue downstream, crisscrossing Battle Branch five times (easy under normal flows) before turning uphill and joining a series of short, named nature trails that offer vertical variation as well as good views of the valley. Stop by the Monarch of the Forest on your return trip.

Miles and Directions

0.0 Leave east from Park Place on the OWASA Trail, a wide track. Descend toward Battle Branch.

0.2 Reach a trail intersection. Here, the Solitary Hill Trail leaves left. Stay straight with the OWASA Trail after soaking in a view from the Stone Terrace.

0.3 Bridge Battle Branch then turn right, joining the singletrack Rainy Day Trail, avoiding the Glandon Drive Access. Climb along a rocky tributary.

0.4 Reach a four-way intersection. Leave right on the Deer Track Trail. Descend in tight-knit woods.

0.5 Leave right on the Sourwood Loop. Here you turn upstream along Battle Branch, passing within sight of the parking area. Curve south along Battle Branch, with Boundary Street to your right. Small cascades drop along Battle Branch.

0.7 Come to a trail intersection and the stone Forest Theater. Join a path along the Forest Theater and rise to a small picnic area and another trailhead. Join the Rainy Day Trail then split right with the University Trail.

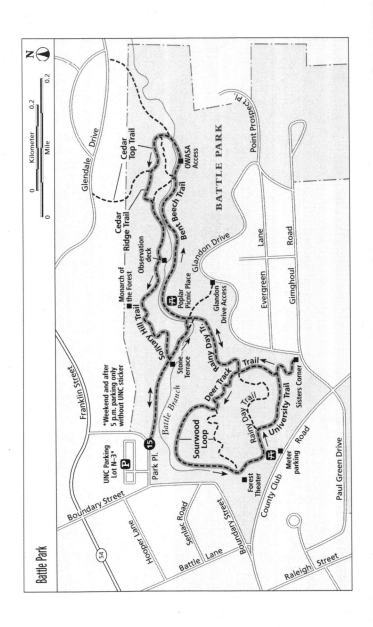

Battle Park

0.8 Take the out-and-back spur to Sisters Corner, then resume the loop, and join the Deer Track Trail. Ahead, split right with the Rainy Day Trail.

1.0 Rejoin the wider OWASA Access. Pass the Poplar Picnic Place then make five creek crossings.

1.5 Split left on the singletrack Cedar Top Trail. Ascend then stay left with the Cedar Ridge Trail. Drop back to meet the Bent Beech Trail. Continue heading upstream.

1.7 Pass an observation deck situated on a bluff above Battle Branch.

1.8 Split right with the Solitary Hill Trail. Look right for the large tulip tree, the Monarch of the Forest, about 80 feet uphill from the trail, set in a draw.

1.9 Complete the Solitary Hill Trail and the second loop. Backtrack on the OWASA Access.

2.1 Return to the Park Place trailhead, finishing the hike.

16 Morgan Creek Trail

This hike mixes a classic streamside greenway with a natural surface loop around a hilly meadow mixed with trees. The hardest part of the hike may be finding the trailhead parking the first time. After making your way to the path's beginning, enjoy a level stroll along big Morgan Creek to reach Merritts Pasture, a large greenspace. From there, climb a hill to enjoy a fine Piedmont vista then circle down Merritts Pasture. From there it is a simple backtrack to the trailhead.

Distance: 2.4-mile balloon loop
Hiking time: 1.5–2.0 hours
Difficulty: Easy
Trail surface: Concrete and natural surface
Best season: Fall through spring
Other trail users: Joggers
Canine compatibility: Leashed dogs permitted
Fees and permits: None

Schedule: Parking lot open Nov–Feb 7 a.m.–6:30 p.m. and Mar–Oct 6 a.m.–9 p.m.
Maps: Morgan Creek Trail Fan Branch Trail; USGS Chapel Hill
Trail contacts: Chapel Hill Parks and Recreation, 200 Plant Rd., Chapel Hill, NC 27514, (919) 968-2784, www.townofchapelhill .org

Finding the trailhead: From the intersection of Smith Level Road/ South Greensboro Road and Fordham Boulevard, south of downtown Chapel Hill, stay east with Fordham Boulevard for 0.6 mile and look for the right turn access for the Morgan Creek Trail/Merritts Pasture parking area, just past the turn into Kingswood Apartments. (**Note:** The parking area is eastbound access only.) Trailhead GPS: N35 53.772', W79 3.865'

The Hike

Morgan Creek is an important stream in the Triangle. Flowing from the shadows of 800-foot Pickards Mountain, Morgan Creek begins its 17-mile southeasterly journey to end at Jordan Lake, having lost 300 feet of elevation along the way. During its course, Morgan Creek and its tributaries drain almost 50 square miles of what is now the suburban Piedmont. Its bottomlands were once agriculturally rich fields for Indians that resided along the stream. The white founders of what became North Carolina found these streamside flats idyllic for growing as well. Not only did the settlers farm the valley but they also erected at least eight gristmills along Morgan Creek, to provide power for now-forgotten pioneer lifeways.

Today the Morgan Creek Valley drains residential streets and neighborhoods, as well as functions as a wildlife corridor and a conduit for sewer lines serving the residential areas within its drainage. Importantly, Morgan Creek is also the primary water source for Chapel Hill and Carrboro, where the stream is dammed as University Lake, west of Chapel Hill. Despite the development within its valley, Morgan Creek also harbors Catawba rhododendron and other plants uncommon in the Piedmont.

Clearly, Morgan Creek is a lot of things to a lot of Triangle residents, and to the local flora and fauna too. To address the pressures under which this stream flows, a philanthropic outfit called the Morgan Creek Valley Alliance has been formed to "promote understanding, conservation, and restoration of Morgan Creek's rich natural resources, beauty, and biological diversity." This group works to preserve the cultural and natural heritage of Morgan Creek both publicly and privately.

As you walk the Morgan Creek Trail, consider the ways clean waters and greenways enhance local life. This greenway leaves the parking area off Fordham Boulevard and heads easterly, out of sight of Morgan Creek. The path meanders through woods and clearings created by a power line, then sidles alongside Morgan Creek and meets the Fan Branch Trail before working under the US 15/US 501 bridge. The level track keeps easterly, bridges a little tributary, then comes to the natural surface Merritts Pasture Trail. Here you continue along Morgan Creek, gaining views of the bluffs across the water before turning away and climbing through woods to the crest of Merritts Pasture. Emerge onto a meadow and enjoy an unexpectedly rewarding view across the Morgan Creek watershed. The last part of the hike returns you to the Morgan Creek Trail and a backtrack to the trailhead.

Miles and Directions

0.0 Leave east from the parking area on a 10-foot-wide concrete trail. Note the bridge and trail going the other way before heading toward Frank Peter Graham Elementary School. For now, wind in and out of woods and under a power line clearing toward Merritts Pasture. Enjoy a wide greenspace.

0.2 Come alongside Morgan Creek. It is about 20 feet wide and a relatively large creek, alternating in pools and shoals.

0.5 Meet the Fan Branch Trail at a bridge spanning Morgan Creek. It heads south to Southern Community Park. Go out on the bridge to grab a good view of the creek. Continue easterly, following the curve of Morgan Creek. Come near US 15/US 501.

0.6 Walk beneath the US 15/US 501 bridge over Morgan Creek. Beyond the span, a bluff rises across the stream.

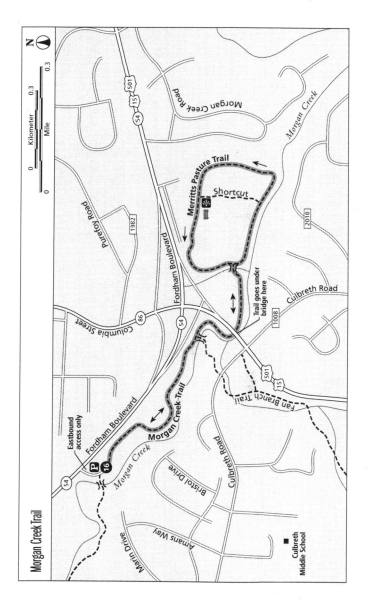

Morgan Creek Trail

0.9 Meet the natural surface Merritts Pasture Trail after bridging a small creek. Stay right here, continuing along Morgan Creek in flats. Pass a shortcut leading left, up an open slope.

1.1 The Merritts Pasture Trail turns away from Morgan Creek and climbs left through hardwoods and pines. A sewer line right-of-way continues down and across Morgan Creek and is closed to the public.

1.3 Meet the other end of the shortcut across Merritts Pasture. A contemplation bench marks a view of the Morgan Creek watershed. Continue on Merritts Pasture Trail, descending in meadow.

1.5 Complete the Merritts Pasture Trail. Bridge the tributary then backtrack westerly.

1.8 Pass under the US 15/US 501 bridge. Curve with Morgan Creek.

1.9 Intersect the Fan Branch Trail on your left.

2.4 Return to the trailhead, completing the hike.

17 Fan Branch Trail

This greenway delivers a little bit of everything, including three creeks to visit. Start the trek at Southern Community Park, where you walk through a wooded preserve before leaving the park near Scroggs Elementary School. Come near Fan Branch as the trail continues north through Southern Village, where it uses the sidewalk along a street for a short period. The trail dips to cross Fan Branch in a widened swath of greenspace then crosses Fan Branch's mother stream—Wilson Creek—twice. Tunnel under Culbreth Road and enter more parkland to meet Morgan Creek and the Morgan Creek Trail.

Distance: 3.6-mile there-and-back

Hiking time: 1.5–2.0 hours

Difficulty: Moderate

Trail surface: Concrete and asphalt

Best season: Fall through spring

Other trail users: Joggers, bicyclers

Canine compatibility: Leashed dogs permitted

Fees and permits: None

Schedule: Dawn to dusk

Maps: Morgan Creek Trail Fan Branch Trail; USGS Farrington, Chapel Hill

Trail contacts: Chapel Hill Parks and Recreation, 200 Plant Rd., Chapel Hill, NC 27514, (919) 968-2784, www.townofchapelhill .org

Finding the trailhead: From the intersection of Fordham Boulevard, Columbia Street, and US 15/US 501 Bypass, south of downtown Chapel Hill, take the US 15/US 501 Bypass south for 1.5 miles to Dogwood Acres Drive and Southern Community Park. (The Dogwood Acres entrance is the second entrance to Southern Community Park you reach. The other, more northerly entrance is Sumac Road.) Turn right on Dogwood Acres Drive and follow it a short distance to enter the dog park and disk golf parking area on your left. Official trailhead address is 1000 Dogwood Acres Dr. Trailhead GPS: N35 52.426', W79 4.156'

The Hike

The greenway system of Chapel Hill is steadily expanding and becoming connected to one another, primarily using wooded strips along the streams that flow through the area. However, to build a greenway trail network you have to incorporate more than just strips of land along waterways. Greenways can also be found in traditional parks and along roads. The Fan Branch Trail uses all the above to make its way from Southern Community Park down to its intersection with the Morgan Creek Trail. Used by hikers, walkers, neighborhood residents, bicyclists, and even schoolchildren, the Fan Branch Trail is not only a recreational path but is used for transportation purposes too, one of the added benefits of a greenway.

The Fan Branch Trail is a good example of how greenways are being incorporated into overall urban planning. Developers and city planners must deal with ever-increasing regulations regarding stormwater runoff, public health and safety, resource protection, and resource management. Adding greenways to developments addresses many questions. For example, a greenway can cut down on stormwater runoff and reduce flooding, which addresses public safety. A greenway helps protect the natural resources of an area. Developing a greenway also enhances overall aesthetics, improving the "quality of place."

The hike starts at Southern Community Park. It not only has the Fan Branch Trail but also an additional natural surface nature trail that makes a short loop. The park is popular with pet lovers as it has a designated dog park area. A disc golf course is integrated into the woods near the trailhead. The park also has a playground, restrooms, and picnic area, including picnic shelters. A basketball court and inline hockey court complete the offerings. The hike enters woods, crossing Dogwood Acres Drive, and winds past the abovementioned courts then curves around Scroggs Elementary School. It then comes alongside Fan Branch, flowing north toward Wilson Creek. You leave the community park, cruising a wooded strip to cross Aberdeen Drive. This is where the trail joins the Southern Village neighborhood, traveling the west side of Edgewater Circle. Fan Branch flows down the hill below, while houses are across the street.

After leaving Southern Village you cross Fan Branch then come to the second stream, Wilson Creek, bridging it twice within the bounds of Culbreth Park. A lighted tunnel leads under Culbreth Road, then the trail opens to bottomland. Soon you are at the third stream, Morgan Creek, with options of extending your trek on the Morgan Creek Trail, heading to the Merritts Pasture Trail, or simply backtracking to the trailhead at Southern Community Park.

Miles and Directions

0.0 Leave north from the parking area near the dog park on an asphalt path. Cross Dogwood Acres Drive. Enter woods as the mostly natural surface, unnamed park nature trail comes in from your left. Stay straight with the Fan Branch Trail. Pass ball courts on your right.

0.2 A spur trail leaves right to Scroggs Elementary School, located on property adjacent to Southern Community Park. Descend toward Fan Branch. Just ahead, pass the other end of the nature trail. It winds back to the trailhead through the

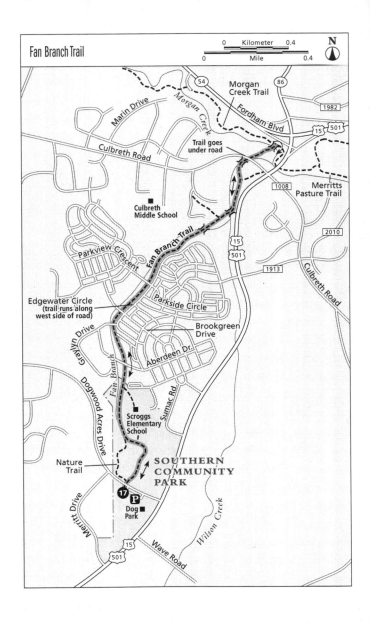

Fan Branch Trail

0 ——— Kilometer ——— 0.4
0 ——— Mile ——— 0.4

N

Morgan Creek Trail

Morgan Creek

Marin Drive

Fordham Blvd

1982

15 501

Culbreth Road

Trail goes under road

1008

Merritts Pasture Trail

Culbreth Middle School

Fan Branch Trail

2010

Parkview Crescent

15 501

1913

Culbreth Road

Edgewater Circle (trail runs along west side of road)

Parkside Circle

Brookgreen Drive

Greylyn Drive

Aberdeen Dr.

Sumac Rd.

Fan Branch

Dogwood Acres Drive

Scroggs Elementary School

SOUTHERN COMMUNITY PARK

Nature Trail

Wilson Creek

Merritt Drive

17 P

Dog Park

15 501

Wave Road

disc golf course and can be challenging to follow since it mixes in with the disc golf holes.

0.5 Pass the second spur to Scroggs Elementary School. Soon leave Southern Community Park.

0.6 Cross Aberdeen Drive, now on a traditional greenway.

0.7 Cross Graylyn Drive at a small playground. The traditional greenway ends, and you now walk a sidewalk on the west side of Edgewater Circle. Houses are across the street while Fan Branch flows below. Ahead, cross Parkview Crescent.

1.1 Break left from the sidewalk of Edgewater Circle. Drop to now-bigger Fan Branch.

1.2 Bridge Fan Branch and enter Culbreth Park, another wide greenspace. Pass a spur leading left to Fan Branch Lane.

1.4 Bridge much bigger Wilson Creek. Turn more northerly, running parallel to US 15/US 501.

1.5 A spur trail leads right, up to US 15/US 501. Cruise through bottomland.

1.6 Bridge Wilson Creek a second time then pass under Culbreth Road in a lighted, short tunnel.

1.8 Reach the bridge over your third creek, Morgan Creek. Meet the Morgan Creek Trail. From here it is 0.5 mile left to the trailhead off Fordham Boulevard and 0.4 mile right to Merritts Pasture Trail. Backtrack.

3.6 Return to the trailhead, completing the hike.

18 Jordan Lake Educational State Forest

Explore an intentionally educational forest situated on a peninsula of Jordan Lake. Here you can enjoy three loop walks. The Lowlands Trail leads by a creek and to a lake cove, then the lake itself. Next, the Talking Trees Trail allows you to learn more about the components of the forest. Finally, the Forest Demonstration Trail offers the longest circuit. Here you can view different forest types and learn about management techniques used to maintain them. It also avails a panorama of Jordan Lake. (**Note:** The forest is open specific times and seasons. Check before you come here.)

Distance: 3.2-mile triple loop
Hiking time: 1.5-2.5 hours
Difficulty: Easy-moderate
Trail surface: Natural
Best season: Spring and fall
Other trail users: Students
Canine compatibility: Leashed dogs permitted
Fees and permits: None
Schedule: Thanksgiving through Jan 30, Mon-Fri 9 a.m.-5 p.m., closed weekends and state holidays; Feb 1 until Thanksgiving, Mon-Fri 9 a.m.-5 p.m., Sat-Sun 11 a.m. to sunset
Maps: Jordan Lake Educational State Forest; USGS Farrington
Trail contacts: Jordan Lake Educational State Forest, 2832 Big Woods Rd., Chapel Hill, NC 27514, (919) 542-1154, www.ncesf.org

Finding the trailhead: From Chapel Hill, take the US 15/US 501 Bypass south to Jack Bennett Road and a traffic light. Turn left on Jack Bennett Road and follow it for 2.4 miles then turn right on Big Woods Road. Follow Big Woods Road for 3.5 miles to the educational forest entrance on your left (not the headquarters entrance).

Continue past the forest office then park in the lot by the restrooms. Official trailhead address is 2832 Big Woods Rd. Trailhead GPS: N35 46.541', W79 2.553'

The Hike

It is no secret in our technologically heavy world that today's children—and adults—are suffering from "nature deficit disorder," simply a disconnection from the natural world. Jordan Lake Educational State Forest helps North Carolina's citizenry not only reconnect with nature but also learn about the forests that impact our world. These state forests are a living outdoor classroom that "teaches children and adults about the complex, interdependent ecosystems which make up a forest and which can be managed for a multitude of uses." School groups, here on a regular basis, are led by a ranger onto the trails to learn more about the forest. You can do the same with yourself, friends, or family.

If you think about it, forests do influence our daily lives. An obvious example is paper. Paper comes from trees and we use paper on a regular basis, not only for writing but also for reading and the transferring of information via pamphlets, maps, menus, and more. Indirectly, trees slow erosion and improve our water supply. In this case the trees here at Jordan Lake Educational State Forest help keep the waters of Jordan Lake clean. Jordan Lake is a major water source for Triangle residents. Forests cool areas in the summer. Trees also add visual beauty to neighborhoods, parks, and shopping centers.

Jordan Lake Educational State Forest has four separate loop trails. Our hike explores three of them. Start on the Lowlands Trail. It leads through pine woods down to a creek. Here you can explore bottomland forest then come alongside a cove of Jordan Lake. Enjoy a watery vista then turn back and walk through re-growing forest and timbered terrain. After backtracking, join the famous Talking Tree Trail. Along the loop—as its name implies—particular trees are "talking trees." Push a button and hear a recorded message that tells thought-provoking information about that tree type. There are several of these talking trees along the trail, and they are a big hit with younger hikers. Adults can learn a thing or two, too.

The Forest Demonstration Trail is by far the longest path and perhaps the most rewarding. First stop by an old homesite then take off down a peninsula. Signage and truly different types of forest show how woodlands are managed. The rolling pine/wiregrass ecosystem is worth the hike itself. Top your learning experience off with a far-reaching view of Jordan Lake then return up the peninsula, curving alongside quiet coves. If you want to extend your hike, simply add on the ¾ mile Wildlife Trail. Finally, consider bringing a picnic, as the forest has a shady picnic area and shelter.

Miles and Directions

0.0 Leave the parking area and restrooms south to the trailhead kiosk. Walk a few feet then turn right on the Lowlands Trail. Curve through pines and behind the picnic shelter. Descend from a hill to bridge an unnamed stream. Watch for rock outcrops.

0.2 Split left with the Lowlands Trail. Curve out along a cove then grab a view of Jordan Lake. Leave the water then come to a timbered area, mixed with regenerating pine.

0.6 Complete the loop portion of the Lowlands Trail. Backtrack.

0.8 Return to the main trail and turn right to soon join the Talking Trees Trail. Pass the wooden Forestry Center building. Begin a clockwise loop, passing the "talking trees."

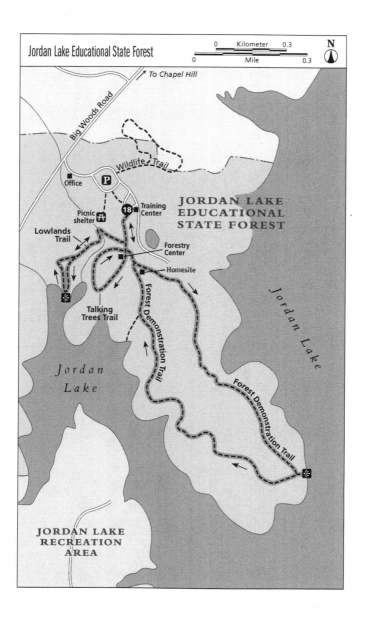

Jordan Lake Educational State Forest

0   Kilometer   0.3

0   Mile   0.3

N

To Chapel Hill

Big Woods Road

Wildlife Trail

Office

P

Picnic shelter

18

Training Center

JORDAN LAKE
EDUCATIONAL
STATE FOREST

Lowlands Trail

Forestry Center

Homesite

Talking Trees Trail

Forest Demonstration Trail

Jordan Lake

Forest Demonstration Trail

Jordan Lake

JORDAN LAKE
RECREATION
AREA

1.1 Complete the Talking Trees Trail loop. Head south and reach the Forest Demonstration Trail. It soon splits; head left and begin the circuit. Note the tin roofing and rock foundation of a homesite. Jonquils and other perennials rise in spring.

1.3 Cross a closed forest road and begin hiking through fire-managed pine/wiregrass woods. Jordan Lake lies to your left. Pass informative signage about forestry practices.

2.0 Take the spur left to a point overlooking Jordan Lake. Soak in big views. Resume the loop, heading west then north, crossing a few forest roads. Come alongside lake coves.

2.9 Stay right at a signed spur leading left to the lake.

3.0 Complete the Forest Demonstration Trail. Backtrack.

3.2 Return to the trailhead, completing the hike.

19 Pond Trail at Seaforth

This is a fun and scenic walk at one of Jordan Lake's more popular day use areas. You will find out why it is called the Pond Trail as it passes three different ponds along the way. However, there is more watery scenery to enjoy as the loop portion of the hike also skirts the shores of Jordan Lake, including traversing a boardwalk that spans the melding of land and water. The swim beach, picnic areas, and boat ramp all beg for additional activities to add to your woodland walk.

Distance: 2.0-mile balloon loop

Hiking time: 1.0-1.5 hours

Difficulty: Easy

Trail surface: Natural

Best season: Fall for colors

Other trail users: None

Canine compatibility: Leashed dogs permitted

Fees and permits: Seasonal entrance fee

Schedule: May, June, July, Aug 8 a.m.–9 p.m.; Sept, Oct, Mar, Apr 8 a.m.–8 p.m.; Nov, Dec, Jan, Feb 8 a.m.–6 p.m.

Maps: Jordan Lake State Recreation Area–Seaforth Area; USGS Merry Oaks

Trail contacts: Jordan Lake State Recreation Area, 280 State Park Rd., Apex, NC 27523, (919) 362-0586, www.ncparks.gov

Finding the trailhead: From Chapel Hill, take the US 15/US 501 Bypass south to Jack Bennett Road and a traffic light. Turn left on Jack Bennett Road and follow it for 2.4 miles then turn right on Big Woods Road. Follow Big Woods Road south to US 64. Turn left and join US 64 east for 0.9 mile to turn right on Seaforth Beach Road (Parkers Creek Road leaves left here). Follow Seaforth Beach Road just a short distance, passing the entrance station to turn left into the large boat ramp parking area. The trailhead is on the southwest

corner of the boat ramp parking area. Trailhead GPS: N35 44.142',
W79 2.233'

The Hike

Since 1981 Jordan Lake State Recreation Area has become
one of North Carolina's most popular state parks. Conve-
niently located to Chapel Hill, Raleigh, and much of the
Triangle, Jordan Lake State Recreation Area has numerous
locales where outdoor enthusiasts can find an outlet for their
activities, whether they are boating, swimming, picnicking,
camping, fishing, or, of course, hiking. Jordan Lake came to
be after extensive flooding from the 1945 Homestead Hurricane. It took a long time for the New Hope Creek valley to
be evacuated, old homes and churches demolished or moved,
forests timbered, new bridges and park facilities erected, plus
the dam built. But now Jordan Lake is an integral part of the
land and lives of those who live around it.

The Seaforth area is located on a long peninsula dividing
the Parkers Creek embayment from the main body of Jordan Lake. US 64 cuts the peninsula in half, with the Parkers
Creek area and its large and spacious campground covering
the north part of the peninsula. Like most of Jordan Lake's
shores, the Seaforth area was once farmland. Along this hike
you will see ponds left over from agricultural days, as well as
evidence of other past land uses.

The hike starts at the huge parking area for the Seaforth
boat ramp. Head south through pines and oaks, wandering
through disturbed land whose prior use is lost to time. Reach
the loop portion of the hike. From here the trail continues
south, leading to a view of the main body of Jordan Lake and
passing its first pond. Enter the picnic area and pop out at a
large picnic shelter. From there keep south, emerging at the

swim beach. At this point you must cross the beach parking area near the restrooms to rejoin the trail. This next segment is the most scenic part of the hike. The level track rolls through enticing woods and nears the shore of Jordan Lake. At one point you join a long boardwalk traversing a wetland where lake and land merge. Come near a second pond then pass a third one where you can also soak in a stellar view of the Parkers Creek arm of Jordan Lake. Cross over the park access road and complete the loop. From there it is a short backtrack to the trailhead.

Miles and Directions

0.0 As you look east at the boat ramps of Seaforth, the Pond Trail leaves right from the southwest corner of the parking lot. Immediately enter tall pine-oak woods on a southbound level track.

0.2 Reach a trail intersection just after passing by some irregular terrain. Whether the land was manipulated due to constructing the facilities at Seaforth or prior to that is conjecture. Leave left, joining the loop portion of the Pond Trail. Turn south toward the picnic area. The main body of Jordan Lake stretches to your left.

0.5 Pass a view of Jordan Lake. Just ahead, skirt a pond that is very close to Jordan Lake.

0.6 Emerge at the picnic shelter. Stay left, joining a path along the shore. Ahead, come to the swim beach. Hike along the swim beach then turn inland on a concrete path, passing restrooms.

0.8 Reenter woods on a singletrack path beside a trail kiosk. Cruise through tall woods, curving north.

1.1 Come to a long boardwalk spanning a brushy wetland.

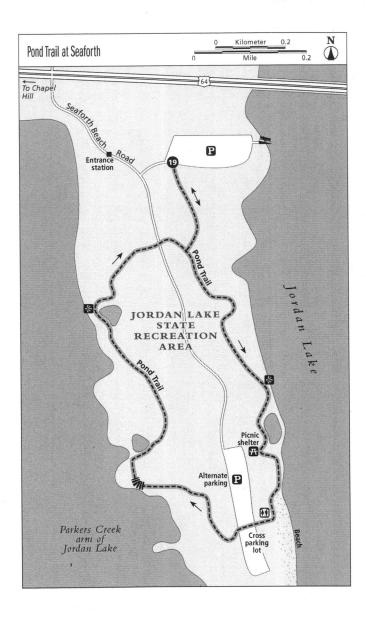

Pond Trail at Seaforth

To Chapel Hill

Seaforth Beach Road

Entrance station

P

19

Pond Trail

JORDAN LAKE
STATE
RECREATION
AREA

Jordan Lake

Pond Trail

Picnic shelter

Alternate parking

P

Parkers Creek
arm of
Jordan Lake

Cross
parking
lot

Beach

Kilometer
Mile

N

1.2 Sidle alongside the second pond, ensconced in pines. The Pond Trail actually uses the berm of the pond for the pathway. Keep north in mostly level woods.

1.5 Reach the third pond. A short path leads left to a waterside view. Skirt the edge of the pond. Compare the water colors of the pond and lake.

1.7 Cross Seaforth Beach Road. Just ahead, complete the loop portion of the hike. Join the spur leading left to the boat ramp parking area.

2.0 Return to the Seaforth boat ramp, completing the hike.

20 Vista Point Loop

This hike combines deep woods walking with added aquatic scenery. Vista Point Recreation Area, on the shores of Jordan Lake, provides a natural setting for this mostly level circuit. From the trailhead you work your way among hollies, pines, and oaks before striking out onto a peninsula surrounded by Jordan Lake. Cruise by a quiet cove before looping around to view the main body of the impoundment. The final part borders little coves before ending at a picnic shelter.

Distance: 2.5-mile loop
Hiking time: 1.5 hours
Difficulty: Easy
Trail surface: Natural
Best season: Year-round
Other trail users: None
Canine compatibility: Leashed dogs permitted
Fees and permits: Seasonal entrance fee

Schedule: May, June, July, Aug 8 a.m.–9 p.m.; Sept, Oct, Mar, Apr 8 a.m.–8 p.m.; Nov, Dec, Jan, Feb 8 a.m.–6 p.m.
Maps: Jordan Lake State Recreation Area–Vista Point; USGS Merry Oaks
Trail contacts: Jordan Lake State Recreation Area, 280 State Park Rd., Apex, NC 27523, (919) 362-0586, www.ncparks.gov

Finding the trailhead: From Chapel Hill, take the US 15/US 501 Bypass south to Jack Bennett Road and a traffic light. Turn left on Jack Bennett Road and follow it for 2.4 miles then turn right on Big Woods Road. Follow Big Woods Road south to US 64. Keep straight here, joining Seaforth Road. Follow Seaforth Road for 1.9 miles to turn left on Pea Ridge Road. Follow Pea Ridge Road 0.7 mile to reach the park and entrance station. Continue past the entrance for 0.8 mile, passing the group tent camping area on your right just before reaching the trailhead on your left. Trailhead GPS: N35 42.294', W79 3.091'

The Hike

For some reason, Jordan Lake State Recreation Area is not very original in their naming of trails. For example, on this hike we follow the Red Trail, with the other trail in the Vista Point area being the Blue Trail. I have a suggestion for renaming the Red Trail. Call it the Holly Trail, for the pathway is flanked with American holly trees along its entire length. You are never too far from a holly on this hike. Hollies are common in North Carolina, from the mountains to the coastal plain. American holly ranges in the East from Pennsylvania down to north-central Florida and west to eastern Texas. However, the humid Southeast—such as the Carolina Piedmont—is where it grows best. This evergreen is easy to identify. Its leaves are spiny, thick, stiff, and leathery, with a dull green color on top and a yellowish green below. Hollies growing in the wild have a treelike form, as opposed to bushes that are cultivated and trimmed in ornamental or hedge fashion in suburban settings. The bark is light gray or tan and often mottled. The bright red berries give the holly its familiar look that makes it a popular decoration during Christmas. Songbirds consume the fruit, as do squirrels, deer, and other small mammals.

Vista Point Recreation Area is located along the western shores of Jordan Lake. It is a quieter parcel of Jordan Lake State Recreation Area, but it does have a large boat ramp, a sailboat launch, a group tent campground, and an RV Group Campground. Vista Point also has two fine trails, one of which is detailed in this hike. Start your walking adventure near the entrance to the group tent campground and enter thick woods. By the way, the lush forest here is very shady in summer, making this a favorable hot weather Piedmont hike.

The woods are flat and can be moist in areas, to the point of vernal pools coming to be during wetter times. Boardwalks help you get across wetter sections of forest. Needles and leaves carpet the trailbed. The Red Trail comes alongside a narrow, scenic bay bordered in woodland. It then heads out a peninsula and curves over to the main body of Jordan Lake. Thus, you get intimate views of the impoundment as well as far-reaching vistas.

Continue along the edge of the peninsula, bridging intermittent streambeds along the way. Some of the streambeds were gullies created when this area was irresponsibly farmed. Forest has taken over the area in its entirety. The path leaves the peninsula, aiming for the concentration of facilities at Vista Point. After passing the RV Group Campground, the trail stops at the picnic shelter. From here make a short road walk to return to the trailhead.

Miles and Directions

0.0   Leave the trailhead kiosk on Pea Ridge Road and enter holly, loblolly pine, and oak flatwoods on the singletrack Red Trail. Boardwalks span moister areas. Look for large cedars too.

0.7   Come within sight of an arm of Jordan Lake. This is a small, narrow bay, showing another side of Jordan Lake. Cruise along the length of the bay.

0.8   A spur leads left to a contemplation bench overlooking the narrow bay. Ahead, continue farther out on a peninsula. The terrain has a little bit of hill to it here. The bay widens.

1.2   Come to another contemplation bench after crossing the peninsula. This view looks east into the main body of Jordan Lake. Pass another good panorama in 0.2 mile. Make an

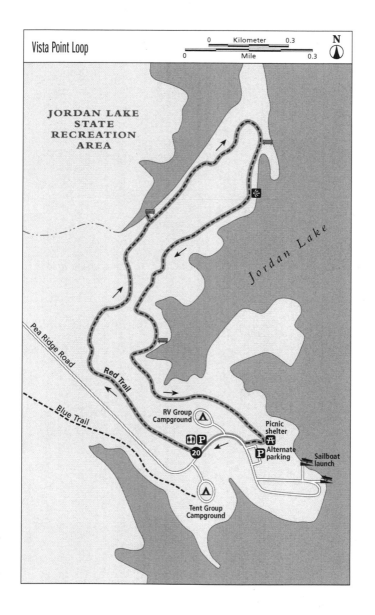

Vista Point Loop

0   Kilometer   0.3
0   Mile   0.3

N

JORDAN LAKE
STATE
RECREATION
AREA

Jordan Lake

Pea Ridge Road

Red Trail

Blue Trail

RV Group
Campground

Picnic
shelter

P Alternate
parking

Sailboat
launch

20

Tent Group
Campground

enjoyable cruise through woods, occasionally crossing a streambed by footbridge in mostly flat forest.

1.9 Pass another contemplation bench as you leave the peninsula.

2.2 Come near the RV Group Campground. Social trails cross the main path, making the area potentially confusing. Stay with the red blazes.

2.4 Reach the Vista Point picnic shelter and the Red Trail's end. From here head out to the main road and take a right. Follow the road back toward the trailhead.

2.5 Return to the trailhead, completing the hike.

About the Author

Native Southerner Johnny Molloy has traveled trails, roads, and waterways of North Carolina and beyond. The avid hiker, cyclist, backpacker, camper, and paddler has authored over 75 outdoor guides covering all or parts of 26 states, focusing on the Southeast. His North Carolina Falcon Guides include *Coastal Trails of the Carolinas*, *Best Hikes Near Asheville, North Carolina*, *Best Outdoor Adventures Asheville*, *Best Easy Day Hikes Greensboro and Winston-Salem*, *Best Hikes Near Raleigh, Durham, and Chapel Hill*. Johnny has camped hundreds of nights in the Tar Heel State from the Outer Banks to the Smoky Mountains and all points between. For more information about Johnny, please visit johnnymolloy.com.